Les Pavillons

FRONTISPIECE: Château de Suisnes

Les Pavillons

FRENCH PAVILIONS OF THE
EIGHTEENTH CENTURY

JEROME ZERBE & CYRIL CONNOLLY

W · W · NORTON & COMPANY

NEW YORK · LONDON

Reprinted with permission of Macmillan Publishing Co., Inc. from
THE PAVILLONS OF EUROPE by Cyril Connolly and Jerome Zerbe
Copyright © 1962 by Cyril Connolly and Jerome Zerbe.

Library of Congress Cataloging in Publication Data

Connolly, Cyril, 1903–1974.
    Les pavillons of the eighteenth century. (Original title: Les Pavillons:
French Pavilions of the eighteenth century)
    1. Pavilions—France. 2. Architecture, Domestic—France.
I. Zerbe, Jerome, 1904–   joint author. II. Title.
NA8450.C58   1979   728   79–19630
                    ISBN 0–393–01279–4

1 2 3 4 5 6 7 8 9 0

ACKNOWLEDGMENTS

Apart from historical memoirs and biographies quoted in the Introduction, and others on Louis XV, XVI, Madame de Pompadour, Madame Du Barry, Madame du Deffand, Mlle. de Lespinasse, the Duc de Lauzun, Diderot's letters, memoirs of the Prince de Ligne, of Marmontel, of Chamfort, Saint Simon, Mercier, Walpole, Delisle, Mme. Geoffrin, and so forth, the author has drawn deeply on the following:

Anciens Châteaux de France: L'Ile de France by J. Vacquier (Paris-Condet, 1913); *Châteaux et Manoirs de France,* Vol. V, *Ile-de-France* by Ernest de Ganay (Vincent, Freal, 1939); *Les Jardins de France* by Ernest de Ganay (Librairie Larousse); *Autour de Paris* (2nd series) by André Hallays (Perrin, 1921); *Abbayes et Châteaux de Paris* by Paul Jarry (Plon, 1947); *Ile de France* by Jacques de la Garde (Arts et Voyages, 1954); *Les Hôtels d'Auteuil du Palais Royal, Les Hôtels des Boulevards à Charonne, Les Hôtels du Faubourg Saint-Germain,* all by George Pillement (Editions Bellenand, 1952, 1953); *Versailles and the Trianons* by G. Van der Kemp (Nicholas Kaye, London, 1958); *Le Petit Trianon* by Leon Rey (Vorms, 1936); *Ange-Jacques Gabriel* by the Comte de Fels (Laurens, 1924); *Claude-Nicolas Ledoux* by Marcel Raval and J. Ch. Moreux (Arts et Métiers Grafiques, 1945); *Francois-Joseph Bélanger* (2 vols.) by Jean Stern (Plon, 1930); *China and Gardens of Europe of the Eighteenth Century* by Osvald Sirén (Ronald Press Company, New York, 1950); *Le Style Louis XV: Origines du Rococo* by Fiske Kimball (Picard et Cie., 1949); *French Architects and Sculptors of the Eighteenth Century* by Lady Dilke (Bell, London, 1900); *Paris* by Henri Bidon (Gallimard, 1937); *Versailles* by Victor Fürst and Louis D'Arcy (Phoenix House, London, 1950); *Louis XVI Furniture* by F. J. B. Watson (Alec Tiranti, London, 1960); *Diary of a Scotch Gardener at the French Court,* edited with an introduction by Francis Birrell (Routledge, London, 1931); *The Hotel de Chanaleilles (Connaissance des Arts,* Nov. 1960); *Le Désert de M. de Monville* by Raymond Lecuyer and J. Ch. Moreux.

C. C.

My sincere thanks are due to all the owners of these places who were kind enough to let me take my photographs; to André Ostier, Peter Fink, Jean Louis Mettetal, and Gerald Van der Kemp who were most helpful, and to Mme. Doussaye and Mlle. Ecker of the French Tourist Bureau who were tireless in my behalf. Also to Pan American Airways who made several of my innumerable trips possible.

J. Z.

FOREWORD

The pavillons, or folies, of the eighteenth century were to European luminaries what our second homes are to us. Indeed, they were more important, since they provided an escape from the trying duties of court life. From pictures of these interiors, we can imagine the style of life that went on within them: a grandee of the period would shuffle the floor, rather than simply walking, as we do. There would be but a limited number of *tabourets* for the privileged to use as seating; all the rest stood.

Plumbing in the folies was scanty by our standards. These houses had very few toilets, even if these were equipped with water tanks and cisterns. The bathtubs for the favored had storage tanks above them, and often a tank was equipped to provide hot water. Clearly, since some three thousand people lived in the small, exquisite rooms of the Palace of Versailles that was blessed with but three hundred bathrooms, plumbing arrangements were far from what we in the twentieth century would call comfortable. Perfume was, thus, a "must" amenity.

The courtiers, who were very rich, would get the finest of architects, the very best of sculptures, painters, and those craftsmen who specialized in fine wood inlay. And so, once one of the folies was finished, it would be comparable in quality to any of the courtiers' rooms in the palace at Versailles, and apt to be far more comfortably arranged at that.

The style and taste of the pavillons have held over the years. Only a handful have become museums. Most are still dwellings and one could live most pleasantly in almost any of them. Cleverly placed conveniences have been fitted into the rooms—refrigerators, phones, and electricity among them—so that most are completely "livable."

It is not everyone's privilege to visit these charming places, and I hope this book will give pleasure to those who cannot and serve as a souvenir to those who can.

Jerome Zerbe

Contents

Les Pavillons

(Above) Le Château de Stors at the end of World War II. (Below) Ruins of Château de Béarn.

Pavane for a Vanished Society

Let us begin with a definition. A 'pavillon' was a tent, then a square tent-shaped room, or the high ends and 'extrémités angulaires' of certain large buildings, hence any building in the garden away from the main house. We take our title from these garden-houses, if big enough to be lived in, and we include certain small châteaux and some town houses which have a particular garden quality and were constructed out of a desire to get away. The English 'country house,' the French 'maison de plaisance,' the German 'lustschloss' convey the same idea but with no limitations as to size, so it is better to stretch the name 'pavilion' to include a few somewhat larger houses—exercises in simplicity.

Folly, in both French and English, suggests a small building which is either bizarre or extravagant and is usually coupled with the name of its creator. But Littré suspects it derives from 'feuilée' or 'feuillie,' a leafy arbor, or branch-house (from the 'foleia' of medieval Latin), with nothing outrageous about it.

The aim of this album is not to provide an exact work of reference so much as to recreate that 'douceur de vivre' of the days before the French Revolution and thus to help the reader to explore this charming world for himself. We have witnessed a major renewal of interest in the eighteenth century and a spectacular boom in the furniture, paintings and minor objects of the reigns of Louis XV and Louis XVI but the houses from which these things were taken have not shared in the general revaluation; perhaps because they cannot be circulated on exhibition or change hands in the auction room. Indeed they show a tendency to disappear, either through war damage or because they are expensive to repair or because the spacious pattern of forecourt and house, with garden behind, inflames the greed of the town planner. Some fall into the hands of devoted private owners, others are kept up by the state but not a few grow ruinous or are taken over by corporate bodies—bureaucratic, military or religious—who find our attentions unwelcome.

I have mentioned the idea of 'getting away' as inherent in these follies and pavilions. Getting away from what? Not from the City, which then had many rural advantages, but from Versailles where the French monarchy had sought to construct a gilded prison for the aristocracy and where the etiquette by which Louis XIV had contrived to tame the feudal nobility and impress the world with the might of God's gerent had become insupportable even to himself. Thus Louis XIV tried to escape, first to Marly, then to the Trianon de Porcelaine and the Grand Trianon while Louis XV rebelled in his turn by creating the Petits Appartements and finally the Petit Trianon which was designed for Madame de Pompadour, and became the last sanctuary of Marie Antoinette. Later on, Madame Du Barry erected the Pavillon de Luciennes as a royal rendez-vous, and the King's grandson, the Comte d'Artois, contrived Bagatelle. Meanwhile many others, noblemen or rich financiers, had thought of building in the countryside which was in easy reach of Paris and of the Court, yet where they could escape its terrible etiquette.

We are always in danger of blurring our view of the past through familiarity. We are

13

so used to the idea of Versailles that we no longer can grasp what an extraordinary conception it was. It is as if everybody of high position were to have to spend most of the year in chilly apartments in Windsor Castle or the White House, where the wine sometimes froze on the tables, where they were dependent entirely on one man's favor, and surrounded by envious schemers who were ready to throw all their weight into making any temporary fall from grace permanent, with rustication to the ancestral estates as the final blow. One observer describes the ancient courtiers, themselves dropping into the grave, inquiring with exaggerated unconcern after the health of some decrepit rival whose place they still coveted. How could distinguished men and their families put up with such total loss of liberty, such humiliating habits of ingratiation? Man is a social animal and we all have something of the courtier in us; we turn toward the sun, but the French aristocracy proved willing to deprive themselves of their personal freedom and independence of spirit for over a century.

Louis XIV rebuilt Versailles when Colbert and his advisers had rejected Bernini's designs for the Louvre as too expensive; he appeared to be separating his Court from his Capital as a temporary measure, hardly aware that he was about to indulge an appetite for building which was quite insatiable and which would enable him to carry incompleted plans about in his head for years, plans involving the layout of vast areas of park and garden that would suddenly fall into place to the astonishment of his Court and the consternation of his exchequer. The marshy and featureless character of the area, so much less suitable, it was thought, for a palace than the terrace of Saint Germain, was also a challenge to a lover of grand designs and incited Louis to create a private universe out of nothing; a city, a palace, an enormous garden and a vast hunting forest and park.

The gardens covered two hundred and thirty acres, the park four thousand and the hunting park fifteen thousand, with a boundary wall twenty-six miles long.

In 1661 he took over the celebrated trio, Le Nôtre, Le Vau and Le Brun who had just finished work at Vaux for the disgraced Fouquet. Designers came and went, hordes of workmen were first coaxed, then coerced and ultimately demoralized. Le Nôtre, Le Vau, Colbert, Gabriel succeeded each other; epidemics ravaged the workmen, contractors made fortunes and later went bankrupt when they were no longer paid but the indefatigable royal building-beetle survived them all.

Louis XV resented the grand style and removed the Escalier des Ambassadeurs to make his 'petits appartements' and after a brief hesitation in Paris under the Regent life went on exactly the same, under a permanent autocracy, a moving staircase of preferment with half the treads sawn through. It would be a nice historical exercise to name the exact year when the normal life of the great city which had persisted all this time under the shadow of Versailles came to predominate, when the center of levity shifted from La Cour to La Ville. At the Revolution we observe the City forcing the monarchs to abandon their residence (October, 1789) but the decisive moment was around 1769–1770 when the Du Barry was taking over, or one might date it from the banishment of Choiseul in 1770, the first minister to be more popular out of office than in. What was happening

14

Detail of the Louis XVI interior at Pavillon Français, Versailles

was that the rich bourgeoisie of Paris, the bankers and Fermiers Généraux were becoming too powerful for their miserable court status and also too critically intelligent. Under Louis XIV, the ablest of all modern monarchs, there was not a noticeable intellectual gap because the most intelligent men of his time were not in open opposition. Racine, Descartes, Boileau, Pascal, La Rochefoucauld, La Fontaine, Molière, La Bruyère, Bossuet, were all "palace-worthy." There was nothing subversive about them. But Louis XV was just clever enough to be suspicious of intellectuals, and after the death in 1764 of Madame de Pompadour, who was certainly a clever woman, the atmosphere of intrigue and inertia became less tempting to them than the turmoil of the Paris of the philosophers. Still a much feared and inscrutable despot, with something sacred about him even in his vices, Louis XV, the gracefully bored, was becoming boring. Considering this in terms of our pavilions, we first note the apparent similarity of those two small and perfect masterpieces, Gabriel's Petit Trianon and Ledoux's Pavillon de Luciennes, built for Madame de Pompadour and Madame Du Barry with only five years in between them—but the first is the crown of a great artist's achievement, the second a younger man's essay in a style which he was soon to abandon for ideological town planning. I should like to illustrate these strictures by a quotation from Mercier, who is writing in 1781 with what we would now call a left-wing bias—

"There is not one of his subjects, be he far or near, who does not want news of the Court and whose eyes do not constantly turn towards the King. Such a one asks himself 'who or what is this man who rules over twenty-four million people and in whose name everything is done?' He is surrounded with all the pleasure opulence can provide, new sensations are thought of so that they may be brought to him; he can enjoy every pleasure, there is no need he is unable to satisfy, he is spared everything even to the forestalling of his own desires. In this exalted position what notion can he form of his own surroundings?

"The atmosphere of a Court stamps itself on a mere footman, on the humblest servant of the household. . . . At Court one edges one's way. A courtier's salute is slight, his interrogation without regard, his step on the parquet is of incomparable lightness.

"Are the polite manners of the Court so renowned because they issue from the stronghold of power itself, or are they due to a taste which is infinitely more refined? Here language is more eloquent, behaviour both simpler and finer, manners easier, the whole tone, even jesting itself, is particularly light and well-bred. But there is little justice in the opinions held, feelings of the heart are inexistent, it is a matter of idle ambition, and an inordinate desire for money without working for it. Here people undertake to make you a bishop, a president, a colonel, an academician. The King, the Queen, and the Royal Princes hold no communication save with nobles or the highest ranks; these form their society exclusively; so one may say that princes leave this world without having spoken with a plebeian. . . . The aristocrat can easily understand the King's mind, gain a knowledge of his character, and sometimes divine his thoughts; but they are none the more advanced for that. At the Palace it is improper to speak of affairs to the King; and this rule covers so much that it needs his Majesty's express wish for a subject to dare enter on details or to broach any subject in its entirety. Rarely is a candid speech permitted— in reality no conversation is held, but a magnificent silence reigns only broken by words that mean nothing.

16

"The art of a prince and of princes generally consists in the distribution of contempt and disdain; it is in apportioning these two ingredients in equal measures that they hold the people of their Court in a kind of stupor. None wants to be disdained, none wants to pass for being out of favour, and he who does not get a word pretends that silence was not unfavourable to him. . . . All their faces, notwithstanding their masks, are unable to hide the cruel passions that devour them." *

But supposing one *were* in favor; one of the few trusted male or female companions of that beautiful royal head. We would have basked in a particular atmosphere of expectation —the inviting glances—the hope of benefits, the consciousness of being at the source of power which gave an edge to the intoxicatingly agreeable atmosphere of this most polished society where nothing unpleasant was ever hinted at and even the royal dismissal *"être remercié"* sounded like a compliment. *"Que dieu vous aie dans sa sainte garde."* One needed a talent for the supplest flattery!

"Madame d'Esparbes, couchant avec Louis XV, le Roi lui dit: Tu as couché avec tous mes sujets—Ah, sire!—Tu as eu le Duc de Choiseul—Il est si puissant!—Le maréchal de Richelieu—Il a tant d'esprit!—Monville—Il a une si belle jambe! A la bonne heure; mais le duc d'Aumont, qui n'a rien de tout cela—Ah, sire! Il est si attaché à votre Majesté." . . .†

The French eighteenth century is a period which we can literally live ourselves into. There is a gallery of memoirs and secret histories, there are faithful portrait-painters like La Tour, sculptors who reveal the sitter's innermost personality, prints which recapture moments of casual intimacy, miniatures, conversation pieces, topical songs with their music, chairs and tables whose ownership can be traced, soft paste porcelain glowing with private jokes, and a pet's corner of well known dogs and parrots. It is a civilization which contains everything we can desire except great literature. The seventeenth century and the nineteenth make up for that, but the one is too formal and remote, the other too chaotic and industrialized to challenge our desirable haven; intellectually simmering, socially bland, aesthetically pleasing, emotionally stimulating, with something about it of the large generous wholesomeness of France herself, rich in fertile produce, infinitely variable in climate, a way of life which neither tyranny nor revolution could radically alter. Beyond the compulsive spenders at Versailles, the extravagant courtiers and the argumentative salons, stretched for league after league the oppressed but magnificent landscape with its cornfields and vineyards, its fish and fowl, its seductive country towns and dignified provincial capitals, its mills, its rivers, its dovecotes and barns and blue-shadowed forests that we recognize in Oudry's illustrations to La Fontaine, in the songs and festivals of the lusty peasants, in the well turned wit and well shaped calves of countless self-made Figaros. I once handled a snuffbox by Van Blarenberghe whose tiny facets depicted the journey

---

* *The Picture of Paris*, translated by Wilfrid Jackson. Routledge, London.
† When Madame d'Esparbes was in bed with Louis XV the King said to her: "You've slept with all my subjects." "Oh, Your Majesty." "You've had the Duc de Choiseul." "He's so powerful." "The Duc de Richelieu." "He's so amusing." "Monville." "He has such a good figure." "Good for him—but the Duc d'Aumont who has none of all that." "Oh, Sir. He is so devoted to your Majesty." Chamfort, *Anecdotes*. (Monville was the builder of the Désert de Retz.)

Ruins of the Chinese Pavillon, Désert de Retz, before its complete destruction

of a group of graceful travelers—the Choiseul retinue perhaps—to their home across a wide river. We see them in their red cloaks, fording the vivid Loire and its sandy islands, or looking in on a village fair, perhaps on the way to Chanteloup where the Duc de Choiseul, banished from the Court after his struggle with Madame Du Barry, erected a pagoda in the forest as a viewpoint for the friends who came to visit him in exile, all that now survives of his great estate, a classic example of pavilion-making with that dash of aggression inseparable from the search for perfection. For even as large palaces, like the castles they replaced, were a demonstration of influence and wealth, so these very small bejeweled buildings snapped their fingers at the age. "The insolence of riches will creep out!" (Dr. Johnson)

There is something oriental about Versailles, about the containment of the whole governing class of a country within a labyrinthine palace, with its observation post the Oeil-de-Boeuf, its secret stairs, the elongated little fingernails scratching on the doors instead of knocking, the smell of urine from the corners which caused the returned émigrés to smart with nostalgia ("Versailles était empuanti d'urine" [Chamfort]), with the affected 'little language' with its peculiar usages and pronunciation, the vast expenditure on dress, the hucksters everywhere—all this seraglio makes one but respect the more the genial long-suffering nation that supported it. Apart from the initial outlay of the first fifty years, the money spent by the kings on their pleasures was not the intolerable drain on the country's resources which the Revolutionaries made it out to be. It was financial incompetence rather than extravagance which ruined the Ancien Régime and its inability ever to get the necessary economic reforms past the vested interests obstructing them. Much that seems to us disastrously lavish grew out of the cheapness of labor and the necessity of finding activities for hordes of retainers who belonged to each family. (A staff of thirty-six was thought the minimum for a grand seigneur's town house.) So before we enter the presence of the kindly bigots and enlightened egotists who built these pavilions we must abandon the robes, the wig and black cap in which posterity likes to sit in judgment on its predecessors and remember that these people were in many ways more rounded and integrated than we are, individualists who knew each other too well to tolerate the slightest humbug. "No one owned to disabling infirmities. When half-dead a man would still be carried out hunting and would have thought it better to die at a ball or at a play than in his bed, with tapers at the head and ugly black priests about him." (Aurore de Saxe) They regarded making life pleasant for each other as an end in itself, and politeness as a vocation, they were warm, courageous and horribly sensible and their easy good taste conceals painfully acquired self-knowledge without either anxiety or self-satisfaction. "On a beau jouer sur les mots" wrote one of them (a king), "je soutiens que je suis bon, moi." If one of these philosophers or men of pleasure or aristocrats or hostesses were to enter the room, we would not feel 'you are going to have your head chopped off in a few years and serve you right' but that we were in the presence of someone with far better manners and intenser emotional reactions than our own, a rarer essence, who also made us feel unaccountably gayer and more worth while to ourselves. "What was it like under the Terror?" someone asked Grimod de la Reynière. "You will hardly believe it, but during all those years not a single good turbot ever came on the market."

19

"Flawless, tremendous actors in an antiquated play,
They march through album after album as through
        the darkness of a wood,
Bearing civilisation, like a mask, from yesterday
        into today—
A civilisation as marvelous, and as far far away
As that of Rameses: the intricately spun
Laws of reason lie burnished like hieroglyphics
        in the sun. . . ."
                            (Frederick Prokosch, *Molière*)

Before returning to Versailles and the royal 'building bug' (as Graf Schönborn called his obsession), we might take a look at that Paris of the eighteenth century which had begun to civilize itself when, after the death of Louis XIV, the Regent had transferred the seat of government for a few brief years to the Palais Royal. From that moment dated the importance of the salons. Four of these succeeded each other as one dynasty and through all of them floated Fontenelle, like a sacred carp. The first was the Marquise de Lambert's. She received every Tuesday and Wednesday from 1710–1733 in her apartment in the Palais Mazarin (now the Bibliothèque Nationale). A writer of maxims, hers was an intellectual salon; one could hardly get into the Academy except through it; she went in entirely for conversation (no cards) and died at the age of eighty-six. Madame de Tencin used to go there to keep an eye on the succession and she obtained it. She was an unfrocked nun from the Dauphiné and after an affair with the Chevalier des Touches gave birth to an illegitimate son who was brought up as a foundling and became the lion of the salons d'Alembert. An unprincipled power-lover, she made money out of Law's speculations and opened her salon with Fontenelle and La Motte, then added Marivaux and others from Mme. de Lambert's until she had for her Tuesdays her celebrated table of seven philosophers. Her 'bêtes' as she called them were each given enough velvet to make a pair of trousers.

"D'une riche et doux tissu nos poètes couverts
Affrontaient, grace à toi, la rigueur des hivers."

Few women came except Madame Geoffrin. "Savez-vous ce que la Geoffrin vient faire ici," she would say. "Elle vient voir ce qu'elle pourra recueillir de mon inventaire." Even so, one day, Madame Geoffrin would find Madame Necker visiting her on the same errand. I think one would have liked Madame de Tencin best; there was something scolding and bossy about Mme. Geoffrin for all her good nature and good sense, and something about Madame du Deffand implacably arid. I quote from Marmontel's description of Madame de Tencin.

"I remember two counsels she gave me: One was to make certain of a living apart from literary success, and to give only my superfluous time to such a lottery. 'Woe to him who expects everything from his pen! Nothing is more precarious. A man who makes shoes is sure of his wage; the man who writes a book or a tragedy is never sure of any-

20

thing.' The other piece of advice was to make friends of women rather than men. 'For by means of women,' she said, 'one does what one likes with men; for they are, some too dissipated, others too absorbed in their own concerns, not to neglect yours; instead of which women think of them, if only for want of occupation. Talk to your woman friend one evening of some business that affects you; the next day at her spinning wheel or her tapestry, she will be dreaming of it, searching in her mind for some means of helping you. But with those whom you think will be helpful, guard yourself well from being anything but a friend; for, between lovers, from the moments clouds appear, and misunderstandings and breakings-off all is lost.' " * It might be Lord Chesterfield speaking.

Hard on her heels came Mme. du Deffand. Born Mlle. de Champrond, she was married at an early age to the Marquis du Deffand from whom she soon separated, mistress for a fortnight of the free-thinking Regent, then of Pont de Veyle and after that for twenty-four years of the Président Hénaut. Her earlier habitués were Voltaire and Montesquieu, then d'Alembert, Diderot, and Helvétius, afterward a few people of high fashion. Her best known apartment was in the Convent of Saint Joseph in the Faubourg Saint Germain where she lived from 1747 to her death in 1780. She fell maternally in love with Horace Walpole in later life and through him made several English friends. She was also a close relative of the Duchesse de Choiseul. Because of her admirable letters to Walpole (she writes the French we speak in dreams) we know almost everything about her. She was the embodiment of the spirit of the age of reason in its concentrated strength and limitation. Driven in on itself by her blindness, hampered by her scrappy education, her intellect buzzes distractedly through her letters, generating an intolerable despair which she sometimes expressed in definitions of ennui. "Vous ne savez pas" (she wrote to Voltaire), "vous ne pouvez pas savoir quel est l'état de ceux qui pensent, qui réfléchissent, qui ont quelque activité et sont, en même temps, sans talent, sans occupation, sans dissipation. Joignez à cela de la délicatesse dans le gôut, un peu de discernement, beaucoup d'amour pour la vérité et je vous soutiendrai qu'il serait heureux pour ceux-là de n'être pas nés." "You have no idea—you can't possibly have any conception of what it is like to think, even to meditate, to have some energy and yet at the same time to have no talent, no occupation, no frivolous pastimes. Add to that a taste that is not easily satisfied, a little discrimination, and a great love of the truth, and I still maintain that it would be better for such people never to have been born." Stripped of her noble accoutrements, she is a precursor of one of Samuel Beckett's impotent bedridden desperadoes receiving a few fellow prisoners of time and boredom as the years pass and the shutters are opened and closed or the screen moved from one side of the room to the other. "Dîtes-moi pourquoi, détestant la vie, je redoute la mort" she wrote to Walpole. She too never forgave her protégée—and lectrice—Mlle. de Lespinasse, for removing d'Alembert and some of her philosophers into what was perhaps the most congenial salon of them all, irradiated by her charm and tact and emotional ardor.

> "Son heureux abandon et ses douces langueurs
>   Son air mélancolique, attiraient tous les coeurs
>   Près d'elle on éprouvait un charme irrésistible;
>   Plus jeune que Geoffrin, elle fut plus sensible."

* *Memoirs of Marmontel,* translated by Brigit Patmore. Routledge, London.

21

When she quarreled with Madame du Deffand Mlle. de Lespinasse took refuge with Madame Geoffrin, thus creating an implacable rift between the two most famous hostesses of the day. Even after her death Madame du Deffand never forgot the treachery, in her eyes, of her young 'lectrice' which cost her the friendship of d'Alembert (who became the testamentary executor of Madame Geoffrin—as she had been to Fontenelle). Writing in 1776 to Horace Walpole she mentions getting a letter from the Comtesse de Boufflers: "je me suis rappelé sa conduite avec feu la demoiselle et mon coeur s'est fermé. Oh! vous avez raison; il faut être de pierre et de glace, et surtout n'estimer assez personne pour y prendre confiance." To aid her young protégée Madame Geoffrin sold her three finest Van Loo's for 36,000 livres to the Empress of Russia, and reinvested in inexpensive Hubert Roberts—who painted some charming pictures of her, including one where she is being read to by her servant while she sits in her high-backed chair and dips a biscuit in a coffee cup. Although she kept something of an international salon, the guests were well chosen—but they had to make an effort themselves in order to create the atmosphere in which her sober excellences bloomed, her crisp intelligence sparkled, the gods arrived. Madame du Deffand was a haughty aristocrat with a first-rate mind, tormented by jealousy and a sense of futility; Madame Geoffrin, highest of high-bourgeoisie, had an admirable character, she was given to endless secret generosities though outwardly conventional, royalty was naturally attracted to her because of some healing ingredient of homely wisdom. She would not defend her friends too vigorously when someone attacked them as "that was the way to irritate the viper and arouse his venom." At fourteen she had married a man of fifty-eight, settled in the Rue Saint Honoré and become the especial friend (after Madame de Tencin) of Fontenelle, the legendary arbiter who could recall meetings with Madame de Sévigné and who died ("Carpe que vous vivez longtemps!") in his hundredth year. "Rich enough to make her house the rendez-vous of art and letters," wrote Marmontel,[*] "and recognising that this was a way of securing amusing company for her old age, and also a distinguished way of living, Madame Geoffrin inaugurated her dinners, one on Monday for artists, the other on Wednesday for writers. It was a remarkable thing that without a smattering of art or literature, this woman who had read or learned nothing save at random, did not feel strange in either company—she was even at home; but she had the good sense to speak only about what she knew well, and to allow speech to the better informed on all else; always politely attentive, never seeming bored, even if she did not understand. She was still more skillful at presiding and watching, keeping uncontrolled spirits well in hand and marking the limits of freedom by a word, a gesture; holding those who wished to go beyond by an irresistible thread. "Allons voilà qui est bien" was usually her signal of prudence to her guests. . . ."

The limits of freedom! Or the frontiers of cowardice? That 'invisible thread' has emptied many a salon since. I suppose Paul Valéry was the only great artist of our own time who could put up with them. Even then there were philosophers, Diderot chief among them, who were never quite salon-trained, who talked too much and threw themselves about, and who preferred a house like the Baron d'Holbach's where one could say absolutely anything, however profound or blasphemous or bawdy, no longer a bow in a string quartet but improvising on one's own. "Vous avez été charmant aujourd'hui," said Mme. Geoffrin to the Abbé Saint Pierre. "Madame, je ne suis qu'un instrument dont vous avez bien joué."

22

* *Memoirs of Marmontel*, translated by Brigit Patmore. Routledge, London.

Yet there was also a loss, for one had to listen to the other improvisers, there was no authoritative "voilà qui est bien." Arguments turned sour and uncensored collective confessions might end in recrimination.

> "Les repas se pressaient pour la semaine entière
> Vous dìniez aujourd'hui chez la Popelinière
> Et demain chez Beaujon . . . jamais chez le traiteur."

The freest of such dinners were then held by the Fermier Général Pelletier, for eight or ten bachelors animated by young Crébillon. Then there were Madame Geoffrin's special little late suppers, 'five or six particular friends, well matched and mutually pleased to be together—the meal was light: commonly a fowl, spinach and an omelette.' Death closed her 'bureau d'esprit' in 1777.

"Les gens du monde, quelque peu estimables qu'ils soient, sont toujours plus amusants que d'autres" maintained Madame du Deffand and we should perhaps look in with her on a normal household as in 1776 she witnesses the famous reopening by the Choiseuls of their palace. "They entertain in their gallery, I don't know if you know it, it's enormous and needs seventy or seventy-two candles to light it, the fireplace is in the middle, there's always a huge fire and stoves at each end but in spite of that one's frozen or else one scorches if one stands near the fire or the stoves, everywhere in between is an ice-box. There's a vast crowd of people, all the beauties, all the young girls, great lords and little ones, a big table in the middle where every kind of game is played, which they call a macédoine, tables for whist, piquet, comet; there are four backgammon boards which split one's ear-drums. Are your parties like these? If so I think you can't go often—It's only being alone that I find worse than such a jam."

The major-domo would steal a glance round the salon and estimate whether there would be forty, sixty or eighty people for dinner. This open house which the Choiseuls kept every night when they were not at Court led to their ruin; the Duke died just in time not to suffer. (1785)

*　　*　　*

Louis XV met Madame de Pompadour in 1745 at the famous ball where he was disguised as a yew tree and she went as Diana. After the victory of Fontenoy she was ensconced in the palace. She furnished three rooms with exquisite taste and lived there till 1751. Her whole reign lasted twenty years.

> "Ci-gît qui fut quinze ans pucelle,
> vingt ans catin, puis huit ans maquerelle."

At first she was too cultivated for the King. She organized performances in the tiny theater (there were only fourteen seats). She sang divinely, danced and acted for him. She was a woman "foncièrement bonne," of strong character and considerable political ability, unfortunately misapplied; she was the last royal mistress really to govern ('après nous le déluge' was her phrase—not the King's) even as the Du Barry was the last favorite to gratify the wildest extravagance. In fact, when we say 'Louis XV' we really mean 'Pompadour,' for the styles of the reign were set by her. She judged verses, studied interior decora-

23

Interior of The Hermitage of Madame de Pompadour, Fontainebleau

tion and printing, carved gems herself and befriended innumerable artists and craftsmen from Voltaire and Boucher to the humble decorators of Sèvres. Boucher was her Court painter and also in charge of the Gobelins tapestries, and her brother, the Marquis de Marigny, was made the equivalent to Minister of Fine Arts. It was he who took the famous voyage to Italy with Cochin and others which put Herculaneum into the picture and set off the neo-classical revival that ended the rococo movement. Madame de Pompadour in fact first laid a restraining hand on the delightful style which had come to birth under the Regent and then led it gently into what we now know as Louis Seize, the decorative simplicity of which we need never get tired—not, at least, until the monotonous deadness of neo-classicism enfeebles it. "Reine et marraine du Rococo," the Goncourts called her, but it was also for her, and to cheer her in her last illness, that Louis XV and Gabriel created the Petit Trianon. Afterwards the King claimed that he had never been in love with her, only with Madame de Chateauroux, and there was certainly some absence of physical sympathy between them, but her love for him was deeper and rarer; without her there might have been no disastrous Austrian alliance, but there would have been no "Louis Quinze" either, a style which produced the most opulent and exhilarating furniture imaginable, the creamy translucence of soft-paste china, the bright pale carpets and tapestries, the contrasting tints of delicate paneling, the whole conception of 'les petits appartements'—the small salon, the library, the bedroom, the boudoir. "Dans le fond de son coeur, elle était des nôtres; elle protégeait les lettres autant qu'elle le pouvait: voilà un beau rêve de fini," wrote Voltaire at her death.

The most characteristic architectural triumphs of the reign of Louis XV were huge squares like the Place de la Concorde (Gabriel) and the Place Stanislas at Nancy, with some of the town planning at Bordeaux and its theater, and churches like Saint Sulpice and the Cathedral of Versailles. The King's greatest success was as a road maker. Madame de Pompadour, however, loved houses and owned in all fourteen, one of which, Bellevue (totally stripped and demolished during the Revolution) was the culminating expression of her period. Crécy, Montretout, then La Celle—Saint Cloud and the Hermitage at Versailles were adopted one after the other, followed by another Hermitage at Compiègne (vanished) and then one by Gabriel at Fontainebleau "the only habitation which she could visit today, without grief" (Nancy Mitford). The King would pretend to go out hunting and spend the whole day there with her, often doing the cooking himself. Except for hunting and sex, the King's chief pleasures—chafing dish cookery, undermining his ministers, making coffee or attar of roses, embroidery, decoration and reading other people's love letters—seem disconcertingly feline. Then came the much altered Hôtel des Reservoirs (Versailles) (architect Lassurance) and the nine-windowed façade of Bellevue (1750) (also by Lassurance) with its sculptures by Pigalle, paneling by Verbeckt and paintings by Van Loo and Boucher. The gardens were elaborate, as always. Next followed the Elysée palace, and Champs which she rented and where some of the original decoration survives. Finally she bought Menars, on the Loire, which she left to her brother, the Marquis de Marigny, and where some grotto work by Soufflot is extant. Into all these houses poured a stream of furniture, carpets, tapestries, statues, scientific objects, gold plate and vast quantities of soft paste china. She dominated the entire production of Sèvres. The china was sold personally by the King; one year an Esterhazy, after being shown round in silence, bought the whole annual production for Hungary; sometimes an aristocrat was caught

(Above) Library, Pavillon de Pompadour, Fontainebleau
(Below) Façade and allée of pollarded plane trees, Pavillon Française, Versailles

pocketing a saucer at the Private View. Her books are more pleasing for the bindings with the familiar three castles from her coat of arms than for what they contain. "Few human beings since the world began," according to Miss Mitford, "can have owned so many beautiful things." She died in 1764.

Ange-Jacques Gabriel, the greatest architect of the reign, was born in 1698 into a closed hereditary community of architects; his father was also famous and related to the Mansards and Robert de Cotte and he himself married the daughter of the chief secretary to the Duc d'Antin, the Minister of Works. By 1734 he was in high favor, collaborating with his father at Versailles and Fontainebleau. By 1749 he was caught up after Lassurance in the pavilion-fever of the King and Madame de Pompadour both at Fontainebleau and in the park of Le Petit Trianon, and by 1751 he was at work on a hunting box, Le Butard, a league away from Versailles. Then came the vanished pavilions of Compiègne and Rambouillet and the little pavilion at Bellevue, Le Brimborion. In 1758 his style was altered by the appearance of Le Roy's *Les Ruines des plus Beaux Monuments de la Grèce* (almost contemporary with Robert Adam's celebrated visit to Diocletian's Palace at Spalato). The result of this new influence was Le Petit Trianon in 1762 which can be considered as the first creation of 'Louis Seize.' Intended for Madame de Pompadour it was used for recreation by Madame Du Barry and then lived in by Marie Antoinette to whom it was an indispensable bolt-hole. (The King had to ask her for admittance.) This, one of the most beautiful buildings in the world, is still the center of a controversy to which we must return later. Then came Gabriel's major works, the Ecole Militaire, the Place de la Concorde with the Rue Royale and the Opera at Versailles. The King's death robbed him of his grandiose project for the reconstruction of all the apartments round the Marble Courtyard. As superintendent of Versailles, he had always worked in close collaboration with the King, and in matters of building, Louis, 'le beau roi,' was both meticulous and imaginative, particularly over the Trianon —buildings, menagerie and park—which were an exact interpretation of his wishes. The Duc de Croÿ describes a toilette of the Marquise where she, Gabriel and the King talked architecture the whole time. The King showed him the little Pavillon Français at Trianon and informed him that that was the new style he should adopt. Money, however, was running out; repairs could not be undertaken. Workmen ("leur désertion," it was reported, "est inévitable et prochaine") were never paid. The Marquis de Marigny wrote desperate letters to the Comptroller, the Abbé Terray. Broken windows could only be replaced with paper, tradesmen's supplies to several royal châteaux were cut off, gardeners were starving, nobody would provide any more wood for stoking the Machine de Marly which raised water from the Seine and supplied all the drinking water to Versailles. On such painful memoranda the Well-beloved made no comment. His views were already known. "Les choses, comme elles sont, dureront autant que moi."

Gabriel died in 1781; his bust by Le Moyne in the Louvre reveals a large sunny authoritative face full of serenity and practical wisdom, a courtier and a man of genius used to getting his own way, but we do not know very much about him, except through his inventories. As superintendent of Versailles and, like his father, first architect of the realm, his influence was enormous—through his authority as Director of the Academy of Architecture and his control of the decoration and garden plans of all these royal buildings. Yet he met with opposition from high-ranking bureaucrats like Madame de Pompadour's uncle and brother who stole some credit. The Place de la Concorde remains his epitaph.

(Above) Octagonal elevation
of du Butard.
(Below) Pavillon
d'Aurore, Sceaux

The controversy about the Petit Trianon is part of a larger issue. Who invented the Louis Seize style? France or England? Let us hear first an orthodox French opinion. "C'est le plus chaste, le plus pur, le plus charmant des pavillons, le mieux proportionné à l'extérieur, le mieux distribué à l'intérieur." (Laborde) "There is neither nobility nor grandeur in its aspect, but in their stead the golden dream of middle-class comfort." (Lady Dilke). Blondel, the leading architectural theorist of the reign lamented the decadence by which private dwellings and their interior decoration had ousted more grandiose public and ecclesiastical conceptions. The very beautiful small octagonal 'Pavillon Français' erected by Gabriel in 1749 when the park of the future Petit Trianon was still part botanical garden and domestic menagerie is criticized, for example, by the Comte de Fels: "La bizarrerie du plan, la lourdeur des détails décoratifs, les groupes d'enfants qui surmontent la balustrade rapellent quelque peu certaines défaillances du goût français au commencement du règne de Louis XV." * It was to be followed up by an open-air dining room, or 'Salon Frais,' a trelliswork partition paved with marble. The King spent a great deal of time in this part of the park, among his hothouses, his attar-making and his botanical specimens. The Petit Trianon was not completely decorated till the year of Madame Du Barry's presentation at Court, only then in 1769 was installed the famous mechanical rising table by Loriot which made it possible to dine without servants. It was in September, 1770, that the King slept there for the first time and it was here that he was taken ill with the fatal fever—eventually diagnosed as smallpox—which led to the Du Barry's banishment. In spite of its small proportions, according to the Comte de Fels, "it has an air of nobility, grandeur and majesty, nothing haughty or severe but on the contrary a welcoming grace and kindly dignity." It benefits enormously from the lovely color of the stone, the delicacy of the ornamentation and the contrasting façades (the west, incidently, faces a typical eighteenth century parterre, the east greets the dawn—an unkempt 'English garden'), and if this indeed be the effect of the immediate impact of Greek art on the genius of Gabriel at the height of his powers, it is a landmark in the history of taste as well as in the enjoyment of living. But it has its critics. "Thus the Petit Trianon, though in France deemed to be a novel style of architecture, combines many ingredients of composition that are derived from out-worn English sources," writes Mr. Lees-Milne in his *Age of Adam*.† "These ingredients were in the eyes of the up-to-date contemporary from Great Britain of archaic type that he would term even pre-Palladian and associate with the country houses of Queen Anne's reign. . . . Again the oeil-de-boeuf windows in the basement draped with swags of ribbons and husks, are in the rococo manner of James Gibbs . . . only in the boudoir of Marie Antoinette would the Englishman familiar with the Adam style recognise features that he considered modern." Mr. Fiske Kimball, late director of the Philadelphia Museum and indispensable authority on the Rococo age thought Gabriel was influenced by English pavilions and rotundas like Chiswick, Mereworth and Stourhead, by books like *Vitruvius Britannicus*, or Morris's *Select Architecture* (1757) and Chambers' *Civil Architecture* (1759). During these years England was waging a successful war against France from which for the first time she emerged richer and more influential than her rival and with a more dynamic group of neoclassical reformers (led by Adam) even than Cochin, Caylus and Soufflot.

Professor Réau of the Sorbonne has challenged the Kimball thesis that England domi-

* *Ange-Jacques Gabriel*, par le Comte de Fels. Laurent, Paris.
† Batsford, London.

nated the neo-classical movement through her victories. Did the German victory in 1871 Prussianise French culture, he argues—quite the opposite. "Peut-on prétendre que le Petit Trianon de Gabriel, d'une grâce à la fois si attique et si française, soit le reflet du style de Robert Adam? Peut-on affirmer que le grand décorateur anglais n'a rien emprunté lui-même à son camerade de jeunesse, Clérisseau? . . . c'est Clérisseau qui a introduit le goût des arabesques et des grotesques à l'antique non seulement en France, mais dans toute l'Europe septentrionale et orientale et même dans les pays anglo-saxons . . . il fit des séjour fréquents et prolongés à Londres." *

Charles-Louis Clérisseau (1722–1820) who went with Robert Adam to Spalato, although seven years older, was his employee rather than his tutor (according to Mr. Lees-Milne) "and never engaged upon a building until he decorated the Villa Albani in 1764" whereas Adam's 'grotesques' appeared at Shardeloes as early as 1759–1761. He was primarily a water-color draftsman and secondly an architect. He was in England from 1764–1768 when the Adam influence was already predominant and probably to learn rather than to teach, like his colleague Bélanger, the architect of Saint-James and Bagatelle, who made drawings of Adam's work at Bowood in 1766. (The newly discovered letters [*Robert Adam and His Circle*, John Fleming, Murray, London] from Robert and James Adam on their Grand Tours prove that Clérisseau was hired as guide, draftsman, and secretary by Robert and then retained by James [at £100 a year] to show them buildings and teach them drawing. He was already [1755–1757] making absurd claims about his influence on them, of which they made short work. He is mentioned as a cicerone and copyist, never as a practical architect. "I found out Clérisseau, Nathaniel, in whom there is no guile, yet there is the utmost knowledge of architecture, of perspective, and of designing and colouring I ever saw or had any conception of. He raised my ideas; he created emulation and fire in my breast. I wished above all things to have him with me at Rome to study close with him and to purchase of his works. What I wished for I obtained. He took a liking to me." February 1755.) I am inclined to think the French are as ungrateful to Mr. Kimball for crediting them with the origins of rococo as they are unhappy at being deprived by his researches of their pre-eminence in the neo-classical. The typical French attitude remains that of Anatole France. "Le style français voulut être antique et, trop heureux pour y parvenir, acquit cette pureté, cette noblesse élégante qu'on remarque particulièrement dans les plans de Gabriel." The two pitfalls of the neo-classical are heaviness and insipidity and we begin to be aware of them even in the last years of Louis XV. With the death of Madame de Pompadour something hard and intelligent goes out, some probity in patronage, a certain tenacity in the perfection of taste.

The Comtesse Du Barry rose from the underworld, not from the ambitious bourgeoisie. She was more beautiful even than Madame de Pompadour, without her brilliant accomplishments but kind, cheerful, unambitious and unresentful; she had more sex appeal combined with an engaging easiness and charm of manner. She pleased the King by her erotic talents, by "making him forget," as he said himself, "that he was nearly sixty." She was as extravagant as Madame de Pompadour, but chiefly over jewelry and her appetites were more limited; she was not devoured by the feverish craving for novelty and great possessions nor did she have to think up so many expensive treats and luxurious surprises for

* *Le Rayonnement de Paris au XVIIIe Siècle.* Laffont, Paris.

her aging lover. Her later years revealed many good qualities which were not perceived through the morning mist of calumny that surrounded her triumphs. To know Madame de Pompadour was to have met one of the most sophisticated end products of an era, many-faceted, brilliant, not without considerable artistic talents and political gifts, a loyal friend and most vindictive enemy, but to greet Madame Du Barry was to be enchanted by superb health and natural good breeding, an easy conversation in which we could all relax. One can hardly picture Madame de Pompadour as anywhere except in her time and place; Madame Du Barry is alive today, at a canasta table in Nassau or warming her long legs in a chalet at Gstaad. Apart from her rooms in the palace she acquired only a house in Versailles and the Château of Louveciennes with its Pavilion, worthy to stand with Trianon or Bagatelle. She had only five years, we must remember, in which to gild her cage; Madame de Pompadour had twenty.

It was in January, 1769, that the grim comedy of her presentation was enacted. In 1770 took place the celebrated fêtes at Versailles for the wedding of the future Louis XVI with Marie Antoinette, the last diplomatic triumph of the fallen Choiseul. First the solemn ceremony in the chapel of the palace, then the great supper in Gabriel's theatre where twenty-two diamond-studded members of the royal family were served while all the nobility watched standing, finally the fiasco of the wedding night (the marriage was not consummated for seven years). A fortune was spent on the fireworks, all Paris roamed through the park (which was in a very dilapidated condition). There was a Court ball which Mercier describes: "The most majestic, the most severely solemn, the most superbly ridiculous thing I have ever witnessed was the *French minuet* danced before the King. One scarcely heard the footfalls of the dancers. A silence . . . there is no rendering the effect of this reverent concentration." There were balls simultaneously in two or three places night after night, open-air theaters in the woods and various royal appearances on the balconies. It was the last of the great Versailles receptions. "Three hundred thousand guests filled the vast gardens which were illuminated by every ingenious device that imagination and taste could conspire to invent. Fireworks of an unbelievable intricacy, some of them requiring forty thousand fuses were set off on the Parterre of Latona. By the Grand Canal blazed the Temple of the Sun, an architectural creation of fire; up and down the canal itself drifted a flotilla of illuminated gondolas . . ." and Mr. Loomis * goes on to quote Taine on the courtiers, "of their kind they were perfect. There was not a gown, not a turn of the head, not a voice or turn of phrase which was not a masterpiece of worldly culture and the distilled quintessence of everything exquisite which the social art has ever elaborated." All the fountains played by the firelight's fitful illuminations and the whole sky was lit up in a magnificent grand finale with thirty thousand rockets (at four thousand louis). Twenty-three years later the contractors and caterers had not been paid.

The tendency to denigrate Madame Du Barry leads us to overlook the fact that the architects and craftsmen she employed were just as remarkable as Madame de Pompadour's, although she could not herself enter so much into their achievement. Fragonard replaces Boucher, Gouthière comes into his own. Gabriel, after redesigning the salons of the Château de Luciennes, gives way to Ledoux, last of the great classical architects and first of the moderns. He was born in 1736 and opened his career with a triumph, the decoration of a

* *Du Barry* by Stanley Loomis. Cape, London; Lippincott, Philadelphia.

31

new café, Le Militaire, in the Rue Saint Honoré. "Tout y est riche, grand, simple et respire la belle et saine antiquité" wrote Fréron. "M. Ledoux annonce les plus rares talents." In 1766 he was reconstructing the Hotel Hallwyl, Rue Michel le Comte and building a group of houses at Eaubonne for a rich family of Fermiers Généraux, the Lenormands de Mezières (relations of Madame de Pompadour's husband) which already revealed his interest in urbanization. Then came the Hôtel d'Uzès and in 1771 the invitation from Madame Du Barry to design the Pavilion at Luciennes as a surprise to entertain the King—like the mysterious Brimborion at Bellevue—this time "une boîte d'écaille et de diamant." The interior was exquisitely decorated by the sculptors Lecomte and Pajou, the painters Drouais, Fragonard and Vien, and the gilt-bronze master Gouthière. After many vicissitudes it was more or less rebuilt by M. Coty before the last war, who raised it by a story. "Les curieux vont en foule à Luciennes voir le pavillon de Mme. la Comtesse Du Barry" wrote a contemporary, "mais n'entre pas qui veut." The King came every day from Marly to "ce sanctuaire de volupté" for some fruit and a glass of Spanish wine. He liked to sit under an old lime on the terrace which we may allow ourselves to think is the one that is still standing. Madame Du Barry served him in her white and rose peignoir. Needless to say "le Sieur Ledoux—jeune architecte qui a beaucoup de talent pour la décoration" was never properly paid. It led, however, to his next commission, the stables in her house at Versailles, which were eventually simplified from his own plan, and to several follies and pavilions in Paris—circa 1780—for the actress La Guimard, for the Espinchel, Tabary and Jarnac families and for the Demoiselles de Saint Germain. This last was on the lines of a little pagan temple, and one of the ladies was said to have died of grief seeing it overbuilt by larger and uglier constructions. It is as well that such sensibility is not contagious. The King's death in 1774 put an end to Ledoux's most successful period which already included his projects for a 'ville idéale,' approved by the King for the Salines de Chaux. The later work of Ledoux, much of which was never carried out or was destroyed, the famous 'propylée's' and octroi-houses of Paris, his Rousseau-like schemes, his heavy fantasies are outside our terms of reference. Like Goya his art falls into two halves, one backward-, one forward-looking, but his tragedy was that he was too old to be more than a precursor to Napoleon who would have proved his perfect patron, releasing all his ambition for grandiose monuments, model-town planning and imaginative creations based on the heavy antique. He has left us only eleven unspoiled examples of his work. After being nearly guillotined, he survived the Revolution and died in 1806. He was too expensive for any but the richest in the land and too turbulent to please them; his utopian ideas were unsuited to a modern revolution. An impassioned, slightly paranoiac perfectionist, doomed never to find the right patron or public, "L'architecte," he wrote, "enlace le spectateur dans la séduction du merveilleux."

Nothing helps us better to understand the past than a small conversation piece. I should like to believe that it will one day be possible to inflate such little masterpieces three-dimensionally so that we enter them stereoscopically and find ourselves literally inside the salon of Madame Geoffrin or Madame du Deffand or hearing Mozart perform for the Princesse de Conti or within the little theater of Versailles when Madame de Pompadour is playing Galatea. We possess such a clue to the Pavilion of Luciennes in the water-color by Moreau le Jeune (now in the Louvre) depicting the opening dinner party given by Madame Du Barry for the King on December 27th, 1771. The room is packed and her friends occupy the little galleries for musicians as well. It is also the inauguration of the New Style, the so-called "Louis Seize." The chairs have round backs and straight legs, the rococo has vanished, the torchères by Pajou are nymphs on classical altars, the table-center is a classical monopteral temple, the ceiling partly coffered and the walls articulated by plain Corinthian pilasters.* So novel and perfect is the furnishing in the pavilion that Mr. Watson does not believe that Madame Du Barry was capable of directing it and assumes there must have been some unknown guiding hand. He suggests the Duc d'Aumont. She was certainly able to direct a party. She can be seen at the center of the table, beside the King, turning to the Duc de Richelieu, beside whom is seated the little Maréchale de Mirepoix. Her Senegalese page, Zamore, who afterwards helped to bring her to the scaffold, is in the left foreground. I should like to have been the courtier of such genial condescension who sits with his back to us, his head turned, his sword so casually arranged, the fine flower of a doomed civilization.

Aiguillon, Maupéou, Chauvelin and the young Vicomte Du Barry were also present. There were only six great ladies invited: Mesdames de Mirepoix, de Valentinois, de Montmorency, de l'Hôpital, d'Aiguillon and de Melet. Her steward Morin (also to be guillotined) directs the proceedings and her monogrammed Sèvres service and her unique gold plate are in evidence. It was for one of the two little salons that Fragonard painted his four idyllic love scenes—"Le Rendez-vous," "La Poursuite," "Les Lettres d'Amour" and "L'Amant Couronné." "Le grand ouvrage de Fragonard est, sans doute, la plus belle série de peintures décoratives du XVIII siècle." For some mysterious reason they were not accepted. The likeliest explanation is that Madame Du Barry interfered too much and the artist took offence. Another that the King was displeased with the resemblance to him, another that they did not fit the measurements, another that they were not sufficiently erotic to amuse le grand Ennuyé. I think he may easily have found them slightly insipid after the series that Boucher had painted for Madame de Pompadour. The paintings remained at Grasse and are now in the Frick collection with the Bouchers from Madame de Pompadour's boudoir at Choisy. There were more Fragonards in the Château de Luciennes itself and here all Madame Du Barry's possessions from Versailles were transported after the King's death. It must have been the most treasure-filled private house since Bellevue; Greuze and Drouais were well patronised and she possessed the Van Dyck of Charles I now in the Louvre, "a family portrait" she admitted modestly, through the connection between the Barrymores and the Du Barrys. It was here that the famous jewel robbery took place and one would like to think that some of her treasures are still buried in the grounds, as she described them in her final effort to stave off execution before she gave that last unhuman cry. Chamfort has an anecdote of a more genial kind. When she expressed a wish to go over from Luciennes and see Le Val, the house of her old enemy Monsieur de Beauvau, Madame de Beauvau thought it would be fun to be there and do the honours. They talked of the reign of Louis XV and Madame Du Barry complained of all the slights which had shown her how much she was personally hated. "Not at all," said Madame de Beauvau, "we simply wanted your job." After this frank admission she asked Madame Du Barry if the King was not very malicious about her and Madame de Grammont (Choiseul's sister). "Oh very!" "Well, what did he say about me, for example?" "Only that you were a stuckup intriguer who made your husband do exactly what

* *Louis Seize Furniture* by F. J. B. Watson. Tiranti, London.

33

you wanted." Monsieur de Beauvau being present the conversation was dropped." * This anecdote reminds us of the pleasant habit of driving over to visit other people's houses, so agreeable to the French, yet one summer evening a few years later she was to see the mob throw the head of her lover, the Duc de Brissac, through the open window of her salon. "This ghastly crime that will leave me in eternal sorrow."

The Comte d'Artois, brother of the Dauphin, builder of the last of our three classic follies, had a happier life. Born in 1757 he had a very good time as a royal younger son, rake and dandy, a more than tolerable exile, and, after the 'retour d'émigration' the satisfaction of becoming King in 1824 on a wave of enthusiasm, until the family predilection for absolute government sent him back into exile. His chief passion, like his grandfather's, was hunting, one which can be indulged in through many vicissitudes. He died in exile in 1836 when his contemporaries, Talleyrand and Lafayette, the two other illustrious survivors from the 'Douceur de Vivre,' were still in power.

As a young man he resembled a Regency buck, fond of betting and racing; he was arrogant, amorous and martial-minded (though not particularly brave) and there were allusions to this at Bagatelle; tents and trophies in the Boiseries and a sphinx said to be a portrait of his faithful but rather formidable mistress, Mlle. de Polastron. One room had mirrors not only on walls and ceiling but on the floor.

The second most important émigré, he passed his exile in raising alliances, armies and money, and making love. "The Comte d'Artois is adored. His frank open face and friendly air attract everyone." After the retour d'émigration ("One Frenchman the More") he became more strait-laced and with plaster and whitewash put the spirit and luxurious letter of Bagatelle behind him. His life spans two civilizations; as a child he was painted by Boucher and Oudry, and in the crisis of 1830 he was the first monarch to use the telegraph.

After the death of Louis XV a wave of prudery swept over the court; Greuze set the tone in painting, statues were covered up. The salons were censored and Houdon's Diana barely escaped. Marie Antoinette stuccoed over the private parts of the gods and heroes at Marly and had a marble chemise thrown over the Venus.

In 1777 the Comte d'Artois, then seventeen years old, is supposed to have wagered Marie Antoinette, his sister-in-law, 100,000 livres that he would receive her in a brand new pavilion within three months and to have won his bet by using his influence to commandeer through the Swiss Guard all the building materials arriving at the gates of Paris. The architect was the delightful François-Joseph Bélanger (1744–1818), the expert on English gardens whose future wife, the actress Mlle. Dervieux, inhabited a ravishing pavilion and garden (Rue Chantereine) given her by the Prince de Soubise. She had once been the mistress of the Comte d'Artois. Bélanger was born in 1744 and visited Lord Shelburne at Bowood about 1766; in 1767 he contributed a project for Lansdowne House Gallery. His next work was a pavilion for Lauraguais (the lover of Sophie Arnould), based on Piranesi. Sophie Arnould recommended him in 1769 to her eccentric, emotional and fearless lover. "Je veux tous mes temples comme mes habits à crédit" ("I want all my temples, like my clothes, on credit"), he wrote to Bélanger and so inaugurated that chronic indebtedness which was the hallmark of those who worked

* A friendly note from M. de Beauvau to Mme. Du Barry at Luciennes quoted by André suggests that they became firm friends.

for princely patrons. He was invited by the Prince de Ligne to modernize the gardens of Beloeil but Sophie Arnould pushed him into the "menus plaisirs" and in 1777 he brought the post of architect to the Comte d'Artois with his approval. There followed Bagatelle.

Bélanger is the most delicious architect of the Louis Seize and all his work as builder, garden-designer or decorator is in supremely good taste, especially does he succeed with those neo-classical houses and anglo-chinese gardens which he designed for actresses and writers like Beaumarchais in the garden-suburbs of Paris or in his buildings and temples for great parks. Although he remained friendly with his great love Sophie Arnould all her life, he married the famous cocotte, Mlle. Dervieux, a discarded mistress of his royal patron. They were married in the prison of Saint Lazare where both were held under suspicion and fortunately delivered by the fall of Robespierre. "Pour moi" . . . he wrote to Sophie, breaking the news . . . "ils m'ont mené, volé, incarceré, marié, en me disant qu'ils me traitaient en bon républicain." Gradually the couple recovered their possessions and Bélanger was doing important work again up to his death in 1818.

Bagatelle cost three millions and nine hundred workmen finished it in sixty-four days. The pavilion was in the new Etruscan style (Bélanger had seen Robert Adam's work in England) and represented a new phase of Louis Seize taste since Luciennes. Like Luciennes it differed considerably from what we see today, the inevitable extra story having been added to make bedrooms, with a balcony replacing the portico. The gardens were planned by Bélanger and laid out by Blaikie, the Scotch gardener whose memoirs, edited by the late Francis Birrell, give such a vivid picture. With its river and rocks in the seventy-acre park it must have been one of the earliest 'jardins anglais' as well as having one of the last parterres. In 1835 it was bought by the future Marquis of Hertford and became the repository for the superb Wallace Collection which imposed constant enlargements.* It was an act of true poetic justice that Bagatelle, the first extravagance of the last Bourbon king of France (no one can feel quite the same about Louis Philippe) should later prove the focal point for the rallying of European taste when Lord Hertford, closely followed by the Rothschilds and the Goncourts, began acquiring the masterpieces—the paintings, the furniture, the statues, the china and the clocks—of the discredited French eighteenth century.

His formidable father, cold rake and imperturbably selfish charmer and political schemer, the Lord Steyne of Thackeray's *Vanity Fair*, had married the spoiled child Mie-Mie, daughter of the Duke of Queensberry and the Marchesa Fagnani. He was also a collector and adviser in picture-buying to the Prince Regent. His unloved son lived abroad with his neglected mother and developed an impenetrable carapace of miserliness and misanthropy for which his anonymous outbidding of kings and emperors at the biggest sales provided a deep satisfaction. "Il faut diablement aimer quelqu'un pour le voir" might have been his motto and was applied also to his possessions, many of which were crated away from the auction room never to be opened. "Men are evil," he told the Goncourts, "and when I die I shall at least have the consolation of never having rendered anyone a service."

He had not always preferred things to people. In youth he had contemplated marriage.

* "I went this morning with Yarmouth to look at his new purchase, Bagatelle, where he is repairing and improving the whole domain. . . . We detected some remains of the fresco painting in the boudoir which were done by the orders of the Comte d'Artois and form a great contrast to the present devout habits of Charles." Raikes's Journal, March, 1836.

"Lord Yarmouth," wrote Lady Granville (Harriet Cavendish) of the future miser in 1832, "has taken to good company and appears at the dinners and balls. He is the greatest pity that ever was. Such powers of being delightful and captivating, *grandes manières*, talents of all kinds, *finesse d'esprit*, all spent in small base coin. He walks among us like a fallen angel, higher and lower than all of us put together . . . one is also told that odd as it is, *money is his great object, being his idol.*" *

There exist photographs of his rooms at Bagatelle crowded with masterpieces from Versailles, of the gardens with famous statues which have been dispersed, and a family group that is particularly evocative. The fourth marquess with his illegitimate son and secretary Sir Richard Wallace and the future Lady Wallace (then his mistress) are sitting in their finery outside the long windows. The Marquess died there in 1870 and made the generous Sir Richard his heir. Bagatelle finally passed to the latter's secretary, Sir John Murray Scott, who sold it to the City of Paris in 1904. The rose garden is on the site of the riding school where the little Prince Imperial used to take his lessons. The summer house from where the Emperor, who was one of the rare visitors, used to watch him still exists. The other constructions to be seen are of the same date. "Parva sed apta." *Little and Right!* The motto (there was no room for 'domus') sums up the whole aesthetic of pavilion-building, from Palladio to the present day.

In England far more architectural freedom was expressed in the Follies erected, because the Gothic revival had introduced from the 1770's an alternative aesthetic and because a more decentralised régime encouraged the fantasies of prosperous local eccentrics. But in the Ile de France the Petit Trianon was something which could not be escaped and every building with which we deal, down to this century, bears witness to it, except the Désert de Retz which is a true Folly in the English sense. Another anomaly is the nearness of every-thing to Versailles or Paris, in consequence of which our main collection of pavilions is con-demned to grow more and more suburban and this renders them more likely to come to harm, besides diminishing the pleasure of the sightseer, who can reach most of them, alas, by taxi. It is no longer possible to combine a visit with the slightest sense of remoteness, although there *are* some out-of-the-way corners of the Ile de France, particularly in the northern forests where the eighteenth century château of Robertval, for example, perched on a hill, retains an air of being in a far province. Nor is it always easy to recapture the particular atmosphere of the Valois that was so dear to Nerval, or of the luminous Ile de France as the Impressionists saw it. After their vicissitudes, the pavilions are now either state-owned or the prized possession of the very rich; even if one or two are for sale they can no longer be snapped up like a manor in the Dordogne or a Provençal 'mas.' The time to get one is just before or just after a war. "In motoring out to visit our group of refugee colonies in the north of Paris I had sometimes passed through a little village near Ecouen. In one of its streets stood a quiet house which I had never noticed but which had not escaped the quick eye of my friend Mrs. Tyler. She stopped one day and asked the con-cierge if by chance it were for sale. The answer was a foregone conclusion: of course it was for sale. Every house in the Northern Suburbs of Paris was to be bought at that darkest moment of the spring of 1918 . . . the little house has never failed me since. As soon as

36

* *Old Q's Daughter: The History of a Strange Family* (revised edition) by Bernard Falk. Hutchinson, London. See also the introductory catalogue to the Wallace Collection.

Temple of Pab, Désert de Retz

I was settled in it, peace and order came back into my life." (Edith Wharton on the Pavillon Colombe.) The Désert de Retz, however, has been empty for long periods because of the extensive repairs which it requires; there is a charming pavilion (de Polignac) for sale in Saint Germain and the superb Pavillon de Sully is also available—at a price. One sometimes sees pathetic remarks in guidebooks and catalogues like "Sauvera-t-on la Folie-Favart, rue de Ménilmontant, et l'exquis pavillon de Julienne, si abîmé déjà aux Gobelins et l'ermitage du Château de Bagnolet à Charonne?" (Héron de Villefosse, 1945). Financiers and the princely protectors of dancers and actresses built many a Pavillon de Rendez-vous which has disappeared, or at best been moved, like the Duc de Richelieu's Pavillon de Hanovre, from the boulevards to Sceaux. Private owners tend to be old-fashioned or at least a little in love with the past and one does not stumble suddenly upon the purely spherical house designed (but never erected) by Ledoux, or the Folly in the form of a snail contemplated by M. Emilio Terry.* I suppose the truly modern equivalent of one of these Follies would be a Mediterranean beach house or a hide-out in the Arizona desert by Frank Lloyd Wright or Mies van der Rohe. The original occupants of the pavilions were not retired people or weekenders and although bent on pleasure they had only four relaxations—conversation, making love, hunting and play. I would like to add reading aloud and music but they were by no means obligatory, although music and pavilions—those sonatinas in stone—have a strong affinity. Conversation certainly came first. "C'est l'art de tout dire sans être mis à la Bastille," wrote the Abbé Galiani. "It was the most free, the most animated, the most brilliant conversation that it was ever possible to hear" recalled the Abbé Morellet—but what exactly did it sound like? † Were there really enough good talkers—or enough good subjects—to go around? How many long rallies in these mixed doubles of the dining table have survived? We possess many hundreds of anecdotes and no good reporting.

Yes—there is one reporter—one writer alone who boswellizes—be it only himself—at the top level—and who puts down exactly the spoken word in salons, at supper, on the stairs on the way up to bed, or while teasing the swans or walking by the river. The three volumes of letters from Diderot to his beloved blue-stocking Sophie Volland give us exactly what was said and read in the world of the Philosophers in the third and crucial quarter of the century. Sometimes we wish they did not, for he lets us in on scenes of complacent vulgarity. Perhaps it was a faintly vulgar relationship—for Diderot emerges as a light good-natured sentimentalist, filling pages with smug insipid love-chat and fatuous anecdotes of château-life, the prisoner of self-indulgence, of being agreeable and of the salons with their gossip, 'tendresses,' 'cochonneries,' easy philosophizing and showing off. Is this the best society could offer? It was, however, just this effusive vulgarity—and his own indifference—that kept him out of the best society. Diderot was considered too Bohemian for the strictest salons, he lacked their tacit desperation. But he spent an enormous time at Grandval with the rich Baron d'Holbach and his pretty wife and her outrageous mother. "Il [Holbach] a de l'originalité dans le ton et dans les idées. Imaginez un satyre gai, piquant, indécent et nerveux, au milieu d'un groupe de figures chastes, molles et délicates.

---

* Reproduced in *Fantastic Art, Dada, Surrealism*. Museum of Modern Art.
† "The women were treated with the most respectful formality; men usually addressed a lady in the third person, and never used the familiar 'tu' even among themselves in her presence. In speaking to her they adopted a lower pitch of tone than when addressing a man. This shade of deference had an effect of indescribable refinement." Gaston Maugras, "The Duc de Lauzun"

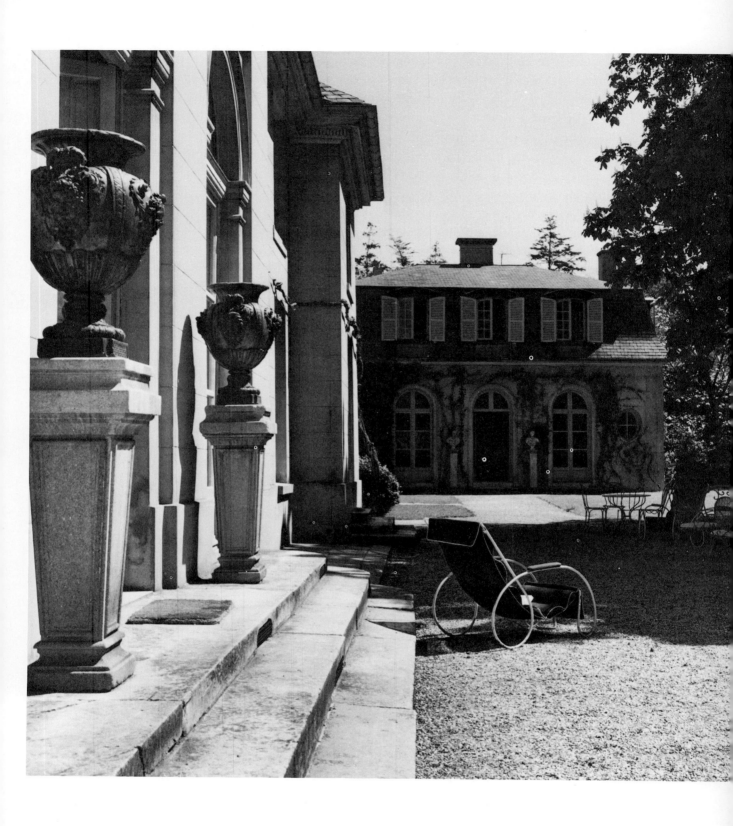

Gravel forecourt of Pavillon Colombe

Tel il était entre nous." Here anything could be said and there was a preoccupation with atheism which was almost obsessive. The *Encyclopaedia* was being written and conversation often consisted of Macaulayesque dissertations on Mahomet or the Chinese interrupted by wise-cracks from the ladies. 'Cochonneries' were welcome; the mother-in-law, Madame d'Aine, has her behind measured against her daughter's and is nearly raped one night on the staircase; she rides the local curé about the salon like a horse and laughs until she makes water all over him (Diderot is beside himself) and at luncheon a wild young man starts plucking the long black hairs off his pretty neighbour's arm. The conversation is like a teen-age debating society breaking up and is carried on with inane self-satisfaction. Although a truly remarkable intelligence, a fount of modern sensibility, a Lamb or Hazlitt in the age of Johnson and bubbling over with mental energy, there is something eager-beaverish about Diderot which loses our respect. He lacks the tragic sense of life, the 'fond noir à contenter'; he is too like ourselves. And yet when he chose he could paint a delightfully objective word picture:

"Nous étions alors dans le triste et magnifique salon, et nous y formions, diversement occupés, un tableau très agréable.

"Vers la fenêtre qui donne sur les jardins, Grim se faisait peindre et Madame d'Epinay était appuyée sur le dos de la chaise de la personne qui le peignait.

"Un dessinateur, assis plus bas, sur un placet faisait son profil au crayon. Il est charmant ce profil; il n'y a point de femme qui ne fut tentée de voir s'il ressemble.

"M. de Saint Lambert lisait dans un coin la dernière brochure que je vous ai envoyée.

"Je jouais aux échecs avec Mme. d'Houdetot. La vielle et bonne Mme. d'Esclarelles, mère de Madame d'Epinay, avait tout autour d'elle tous ses enfants, et causait avec eux et avec leurs gouverneurs.

"Deux soeurs de la personne qui peignait mon ami brodaient, l'une à la main, l'autre au tambour.

"Et une troisième essayait au clavecin une pièce de Scarlatti. . . ."

But that was at Madame d'Epinay's among the Montmorency set, at La Chevrette with its wonderful ices, and not in the grosser atmosphere of Grandval with its 'furious eels,' its melons and choucroute, partridges and pâtés. "Vous comprenez tout ce que cela doit devenir à table au dessert, entre douze et quinze personnes, avec du vin de Champagne, de la gaiété, de l'esprit, et toute la liberté des champs. Madame Geoffrin fut fort bien. Je remarque toujours le goût noble et simple dont cette femme s'habille. . . . M. Schistre quitta sa mandore, et la vivacité de notre plaisir devint le sujet de la conversation. . . . La conversation en prit un tour un peu sérieux. On parla de l'horreur que nous avons tous pour l'anéantissement." *

Perhaps one is jealous, for today our blue-haired, 'neatened up' society is too ill organised to enjoy a discussion on annihilation, on what Madame Geoffrin called "la cessation d'être"; we dare not even meet the same people every day lest we watch each other grow old. Take away the Baron d'Holbach's comic mother-in-law, and our dream of the 'douceur de vivre' reasserts itself around that ebullient philosopher.

* "You can imagine where we had all got to by the time we had reached the fruit, with twelve or fifteen of us, champagne, gaiety, wit and everyone completely outspoken; Madame Geoffrin was in fine form, I am always astounded by the dignified simplicity of her appearance. . . . Monsieur Schistre put aside his mandola and everyone discussed the particular pleasure his playing had caused us. Later on the conversation took a more serious turn and we spoke of the horror which we all felt at our inevitable dissolution."

(Above) Dining room, Pavillon de Sully
(Below) Désert de Retz as it appeared in 1978

"This is how I spend my time. At eight o'clock, dark or light, I get up. I have my two cups of tea. Fair weather or foul, I open my window and take the air. Then I shut myself up and read. . . . Those writers who can charm away our boredom, who ravish us from ourselves, whom nature has endowed with a magic wand which no sooner touches us than we forget our troubles and the light enters the dark places of the soul and we are reconciled to living—they are the only true benefactors of humanity.

"We meet round the fire and go into luncheon after talking for a bit. We always spend a long time over luncheon. Afterwards we go for a walk, or play billiards, or a game of chess.

"Then a little reading and conversation. Piquet, supper and some fooling while we take our candles up, and so to bed."

In summer there were long expeditions with more philosophical discussions. "Le coucher du soleil et la fraîcheur de la soirée nous raprochent de la maison, où nous n'arrivons guère avant sept heures. Les femmes sont rentrées et deshabillées. Il y a des lumières et des cartes sur une table." *

Even the sociable Diderot was sensitive to the past and he has used his magic wand to leave us a charming memory of the vanished Marly (Le Nôtre, Mansart), the second home of Louis XIV where (according to the courtiers) it never rained, and where the statues were castrated by Marie Antoinette (one should look on these statues, wrote Diderot, as people who love solitude and have sought it out, poets, philosophers or lovers, whose privacy is to be respected).

"How sublime it all is—what a mind conceived these gardens—in the highest spot, in two large open spaces to right and left are two enormous octagonal reservoirs, each side a hundred and fifty paces long and so twelve hundred all round. They are reached by dark forgotten alleys, and we only see these vast pieces of water when we are right upon them. And these dark forgotten alleys are ornamented with sad and serious statues—a bronze Laocoon and his children enlaced and eaten by the serpents of Diana. This father in his agony, this dying child and the other who forgets his own danger to watch the sufferings of his father—all those depressed me enormously and my melancholy accorded perfectly with the character of the surroundings. We also saw the state apartments. The main building faces the gardens and represents the palace of the Sun. Twelve isolated pavilions, half buried in the forest in a circle round the garden represent the signs of the Zodiac. The proportions of everything are so perfect that the central pavilion seems of an ordinary size but when you come to measure it the length is 4900 paces. Only when you open the doors do you realise its height and extent. The centre is occupied by one of the most beautiful rooms imaginable. I went in, and when I was in the middle, I reflected that here it was that the Sun King went once a year to overthrow the prosperity of two or three of his courtiers by the turn of a card. . . ."

It might be Angkor; and is it not surprising that Diderot can so admire the work of Le Nôtre (for he went back again) when he was one of the first to enthuse over the Jardins Anglais? One wishes he had given us more accounts of buildings too, judging by what he wrote of Maisons.

"C'est une architecture tout simple. Il est impossible de voir les portes et des croisées de

42

* "Sunset and the cool of the evening bring us home; we seldom get back before seven o'clock; the ladies have already come in and dressed, and the lights are lit round the card tables."

Principal façade of Folie Saint James

meilleur gôut. . . . Avec la simplicité, partout on est touché de l'élégance, de la noblesse et de la légereté. Même caractère dans les jardins. . . . Peu ou point d'arbres taillés; peu ou point de boulingrins; des choses naturelles et agrestes. On voit la rivière d'un côté; de l'autre, la vue se porte sur des montagnes. Une sensation que je n'ai eprouvée que là, c'est que plus j'y demeurais, plus je m'y plaisais; plus je regardais plus j'admirais, parce que je retrouvais jusques dans les plus petites choses, jusques dans les grilles, cette convenance de la demeure avec le rang et le caractère de l'homme." *

We are back again at the true nature of pavilion appeal; 'Parva sed apta.'

* * *

A word about such gardens. In the eighteenth century gardening underwent three styles —the classical—deriving from Le Nôtre, in which man is master of the environment—such were the original gardens of Trianon and everywhere before the 1760's—parterres, bosquets, clipped gardens and avenues, 'boulingrins,' fountains and cascades, statues and vases—as we still see them at Vaux, Versailles, Chantilly and Dampierre. Then came the Jardin Anglais and Jardin Anglo-Chinois, finally the Romantic garden, with a return to classicism much later on. The Jardin Anglais or landscaped garden is not romantic—man is master but conceals his mastery of the environment by shaping and directing Nature from behind the scenes. Madame de Pompadour had created some of the most typical French eighteenth century gardens, in the style of Lajoue of which Bellevue, with its elaborate rococo 'treillages' was the finest, and her intendant Collin's another on a smaller scale. At Luciennes Madame Du Barry had a fine grass parterre bordered by flower beds (in royal gardens new flowers were bedded out once and sometimes twice a day), the Pavillon Colombe at Sainte Brice was also renowned for its trelliswork and statues. Almost the last formal garden was laid at Bagatelle. These geometrical gardens, 'petits appartements' in hornbeam, like the great rides and vistas of Le Nôtre eventually became symbols of the Ancien Régime, anathema to all progressives. All through the century the idea of the 'picturesque' had been seeping through from England (Kent, Brown, Walpole—later Repton and Payne Knight) to join up with the notions of Rousseau, but it was still a step from the cunningly directed landscape gardening of Kent or the Chinese thickets and meanders of Repton to the romantic 'wilderness' with its contemplative ruins. Here man no longer dominates: our species feigns extinction. All the philosophers chimed in—Rousseau, Diderot, Walpole, the Prince de Ligne ("Down with Compasses") even Voltaire who wrote:

Jardins, il faut que je vous fuie
Trop d'art me revolte et m'ennuie
J'aime mieux ces vastes forêts, etc.

Bridgman, Kent, Brown, Whately lead up to Caraman (working for the Duc de Chartres [Egalité] at Monceau, and the expert Prince de Ligne). Bélanger laid out the new 'jardin anglais' at Bagatelle and also the gardens of the Folie St. James, with its enormous rock.

* "It's a perfectly simple style. You can't imagine doors or windows in better taste, and besides its simplicity, one is affected by the distinction, the nobility of conception, and lightness of touch. The same qualities in the gardens. Little or no pollarded trees, hardly any lawns, everything natural and rustic with river to draw the eye on one side and the hills on the other. Something I felt there which I had not felt anywhere else, that the more I lived there, the more I would want to live there; the more I gazed, the more I should admire; because I found even down to the smallest detail, even in the ironwork, that harmony and proportion between the building itself and the character and social position of its owner."

Marie Antoinette anglicized the Trianons with Caraman and Mique, and Blaikie, the Scotch gardener, worked at Bagatelle, Raincy, Maupertuis and others. The most elaborate was at Ermenonville with the tomb of Rousseau (1778) designed by Hubert Robert. The owner, M. de Girardin had visited all the best English gardens, and inscriptions and 'fabriques' are everywhere, designed to create in the beholder the appropriate mood. At Franconville the Picturesque and Romantic had become an open-air museum for the Comte d'Albon. The Désert de Retz pales before the two supreme examples of Méréville (Laborde and Hubert Robert) and Betz (Princesse de Monaco) with rivers, ravines and 'fabriques' on a superb scale. According to Chateaubriand, every émigré returned with the seeds of a tiny 'English garden' in him. Curves were simultaneously banished from rooms and buildings and straight lines from the landscape. The park became a symbol of liberty instead of order. Many owners were Orléanists who avoided the Court and who imported English gardeners, jockeys, and political opinions and men like Bélanger combined the picturesque with the neo-classical into a finale of perfect harmony which the Revolution shattered.

"Le peuple a tout brisé dans sa juste fureur."

*   *   *

Our list does not pretend to be complete: there exist many lesser known pavilions and sometimes they are taken down and put up somewhere else (Méréville has moved to Jeurre), which robs them of their confidence. Others are border-line cases like the Pavillon de Chartres at Monceau which was really one of Ledoux's octroi-houses where the Duke of Orléans kept a room. On the whole our definition of a pavilion is like the Michelin Guide's description of certain modest restaurants: *Où on peut dîner et eventuellement coucher*. This excludes 'fabriques'—the Chinese temples and hermits' grottos, obelisks and cenotaphs, ice-houses, rustic bridges and ruined arches which were meant not to be lived in but to be meditated on, even if as beautiful as Le Roy's Temple of Friendship at Betz or Bélanger's Laiterie at Méréville. Fortunately, my colleague's habit of wearing his lens on his sleeve goes back a very long way and enables us to include some presently inhospitable interiors and exteriors now dilapidated at their most favorable moment.

EDITOR'S NOTE TO 1979 EDITION

A total of forty-six new halftone photographs—some of which Mr. Zerbe made during a recent trip to France—have been added to this edition. Some of the new illustrations have been placed in Mr. Connolly's Introduction and some are in the sections for the individual pavilions.

The Pavillon de Sully

The Pavillon de Sully at St. Germain has the advantage of being built on a steep hillside; above it is the terrace with the château: below the ground falls abruptly to the Seine and the houses of Pecq, providing a wonderful view and a garden of descending terraces. From above the pavilion looks like a high-pooped galleon moored on a lake of gravel. It is approached between two cottagelike buildings which provide staff and guest accommodation while across the main first terrace with clipped yews and a parterre of box stands the isolated pavilion. The effect is immensely graceful, and seems to have no connection with the heavy château above (restored by Napoleon III). In the past, vineyards covered the hillside and the hanging gardens rivaled the Villa d'Este at Tivoli; the whole area was developed round the Pavillon Henri Quatre in the style of the French Renaissance. By the time of Louis XIII, there were two pavilions, one for the chief painter, one for the head gardener of the château with the hanging gardens below them and their elaborate grottoes and water-works. The two pavilions were connected by galleries with the enormous buildings of the main château from which they projected out on each side. It is the head gardener's which is the Pavillon de Sully, the other having disappeared. Although it has only two floors, the pavilion can claim four more underneath, since the wall between each terrace and the next is honeycombed with grottoes and cellars. The windows of one of these, a shady summer dining room, can be seen, creeper-clad, in the illustration. The beautiful water-sculptures and fountains have all gone. Louis XIII as a child used to turn them on to soak his guests. The Château Neuf and its dependencies were largely pulled down by the young Comte d'Artois (Charles X), the builder of Bagatelle, to which some of the statues were removed. Bélanger made plans for remodeling the gardens. At present a descending wall divides the garden in half. On one side is a steep bank of grass in the English style with some fine trees, on the other a formal Tuscan garden recalling the old. A square walled vegetable garden at the bottom unites them. There are three rooms on the ground floor of the pavilion, with a fine bedroom and suite above these, which Madame Mackie has packed with treasures, including a painting of Louis XIV with the château in the background. (He was *not* born in the pavilion but in an apartment [now destroyed] adjoining the Pavillon Henri Quatre up the hill. The name 'de Sully' is only by association of ideas with *Henri Quatre*. The new lease of life of the pavilion dates from its acquisition by M. Paraf in 1899 for 19,000 francs and, after 1918 by M. Delaroche-Vernet. The gardens were restored by M. Claude Dondel.

46

49

Château de la Villette

The Château de la Villette is a small château near Meulan of the time of Louis XIV. The architect was probably J. H. Mansard. It was built for the Comte d'Aufflay, Louis XIV's ambassador to Venice, in 1668 on older foundations, including a sixteenth century pillar (see the illustration), then transformed by Pierre Cousin in 1693 (chapel of 1697). The two side pavilions are also seventeenth century but the wrought-iron gates are eighteenth century and the lime avenues date from 1749. The interior decorations are eighteenth century, the great octagonal salon in white and blue has dessus-de-portes by Boucher. There are two other salons (one with boiseries), and an extremely fine dining room with a carved stone buffet (already there in 1697), a fine chimney piece of 1748, magnificent boiseries in 'Bois de Hollande' by Bouquelet or Duteille and panels by Huché and Desloches (1747). "La salle-à-manger de Villette est d'une rare élégance; c'est un témoin precieux pour l'histoire de l'art décoratif du XVII$_{me}$ et XVIII$_e$ siècles" (Ernest de Ganay). During the eighteenth century the château belonged to the Grouchy family and was considered a little earthly paradise "d'un paysage délicieux, une société charmante, tous les talents réunis à la beauté dans la personne des filles de la maison, la musique, la peinture, le Latin, le Grec, toutes les langues, toutes les sciences." One of these daughters married Condorcet, another Cabanis. Marshal Grouchy (of Waterloo fame) sold the château in 1816. In 1838 it came to the daughter of Fouché and now belongs to M. Robert Gérard who has restored the 'French gardens' as a park according to the old plans.

The Maison de Sylvie

The Maison de Sylvie in the park of Chantilly (originally 1604) is a low stone bungalow, prettier on the garden side, which was rebuilt by Condé the Great in 1684. 'Sylvie' was the name given to Marie Felice Orsini, Duchess of Montmorency, by the Gascon poet Théophile de Viau who was condemned to be burned at the stake by the Parliament of Paris in 1623 for his loose living and licentious verses (he was supposed to be the author of *Le Parnasse Satyrique*) and was hidden by the Duchess in this building. In gratitude he composed ten insipid odes for her. Here is one verse:

> "Je penchais mes yeux sur le bord
> Du lit où la Naïade dort
> Et régardant pêcher Sylvie,
> Je voyais battre les poissons
> A quis plus tôt perdront la vie
> En l'honneur de ses hameçons."

In 1724 the pavilion with its little park was the scene of the romantic love affair of Mlle. de Clermont, sister of the Duc de Bourbon and the Duc de Melun, who was killed in a hunting accident. (There is no connection with the 'Sylvie' of Gerard de Nerval's beautiful 'souvenir du Valois.') The pavilion now contains Chinese curios, tapestries and wood carvings. The busts in front are of Ceres and Bacchus with some lines of Viau engraved by order of the Duc d'Aumale on black marble in the middle. From 1788 to 1814 it was used as a barracks. The Duc d'Aumale added the rotunda, the paneling of which came from a hunting pavilion at Dreux.

The Pavillon de Hanovre

The Pavillon de Hanovre is one of the few survivors of the 'folies d'amour'—'pavillons de rendez-vous' which sprang up all over Paris for the installation of the mistresses of the great. The Duke de Richelieu, the most successful rake and accomplished courtier of the eighteenth century, had several of these in different quarters; the best known being in the Rue de Clichy, where the Casino de Paris now stands. At fifteen he was caught making too free with the Duchess of Burgundy (then aged twelve) on the balcony at Marly; as a very old man the secret police still chronicled his prowess in the brothels; he died aged ninety-eight, cynical, polished, insolvent, leaving boxes of unopened love letters demanding rendez-vous. The pavilion (1760) was built by Chevautet on the Boulevard des Italiens for the Duke from the proceeds, it was said, of his looting in Hanover which he overran in the Seven Years' War. After 1780 it became the Café Velloni and many parties were given there. Its last occupants were Messrs. Christofle and in 1930 it was removed with much hypocrisy to the bottom of the Park of Sceaux to make room for a building as hideous as the other was beautiful. How delicious it must have been, at the end of one of the Duke's 'soupers académiques,' where everyone had changed clothes and mistresses, to step out on to its curving balcony to breathe the dawn. Though Madame Geoffrin would not receive him and called him the 'épluchure des grands vices,' it was said that no salon could be a success unless it included the Duc de Richelieu. I cannot believe that he can confer the same éclat on the Park of Sceaux. Under Louis Philippe the Boulevard des Italiens was the center of Paris. At the corner of the Rue Lafitte Lord Hertford and his brother, Lord Henry Seymour, were installed, with the Rothschilds further up. The Café de Paris, the Café Tortoni, the Chinese Baths, the Maison Doré, the Café Anglais and the Jockey Club were other attractions of the Boulevard—"l'agiotage, le journalisme, la môde, la galanterie, la littérature, l'art, la science, l'aristocratie et la prostitution" swept by the café chairs. (The Café Hardy was the first place in Paris to serve snack luncheons.) There stood, not a stone's throw from the home of the future owner of Bagatelle, "Le Pavillon de Hanovre qui fut baptisé ainsi par la dédaigneuse justice du peuple."

The Pavillon d'Aurore

The Pavillon d'Aurore in the park of Sceaux is one of the buildings remaining from the time of the Minister Colbert, about 1673. Lebrun painted the ceiling which shows Aurore as rosy-fingered Dawn in a chariot with four white horses, accompanied by Summer as she puts to flight Night, in the guise of a bat. The little pavilion, once celebrated for musical entertainments, has been completely restored, and is now used again for that purpose.

The Pavillon du Régent ou de l'Hermitage

The Pavillon du Régent ou de l'Hermitage, 148–50 Rue Bagnolet, Paris (20), once formed a dependency of the Château de Bagnolet (1719) which belonged to the Duchess of Orleans and her son, the Regent, who enlarged it in 1727. The Regent's son had little use for it. His grandson added a theater and died there in 1785 leaving it to his son, Philip Egalité, who was guillotined in 1793. The château was demolished but the Pavillon de l'Hermitage remained. The architect was Serin. This elegant pavilion consisted of a large salon, rounded at one end, and an octagonal vestibule. There were some smaller rooms, a gallery and a little belvedere. The salon was decorated in 'grisaille brune' with a series of panels representing the Temptation of Saint Anthony by Valade—some of these temptations (which still survive) were thought to be excessive. The pavilion was acquired for his mistress, the comic actress Grandmaison, by the Royalist plotter, the Baron de Batz who tried to rescue Louis XVI and Marie Antoinette. He escaped but the actress was guillotined. It is now the property of the Foundation Debrousse.

The Château des Ternes

The Château des Ternes, 19 Rue Demours, is not improved by having had a street pierced through it by an unworthy owner (Lenoir) in 1721 (Rue Bayen). It was built in 1715 by the Treasurer Mirey de Pomponne round a noble courtyard and in the center of a fine park which all later belonged to the brother of Madame d'Houdetot and brother-in-law of Madame d'Epinay. It is the last of the old châteaux in Paris.

The Pavillon Favart

The Pavillon Favart in the Rue de Ménilmontant was the home of the director Favart who lived there from when it was built in 1759 to 1792 with his actress wife, her lover the Abbé de Voisenin and their friends. It now belongs to a religious order and is therefore one of the hardest pavilions to get into. Its very fine façade with tall columns and pediment remind one of similar villas in London or Bath and we see at once its kinship with certain classical plantation houses in America.

The Château de Béarn

The Chateau de Béarn at Saint Cloud is now a ruin (it was burned during the siege of Paris) with a terraced garden which enjoys a marvelous view across the Bois extending from Montmartre to the Invalides. There are some fine trees and a pond with a powerful fountain and a 'théâtre de verdure' whose wings and coulisses are tunnels of pleached hornbeam, including even dressing rooms, and giving on to the grass stage, the whole in a state of romantic decay. The house was built in 1713 for the Elector of Bavaria, Maximilian-Emmanuel while an exile. He had been living at Compiègne on Louis XIV's bounty and was a heavy borrower. Boffrand arranged the apartments. When the Elector returned to Munich it went to a mistress of the Regent, Madame d'Averne, and then to the Prince and Princesse de Carignan. The Prince left six million in debts. In 1749 it was bought by Chalut de Vérins who rebuilt the château, in the style in which it was eventually burned down. His architect was probably Brizeux. In 1786 he let it to the Comtesse d'Artois (known as 'gna-gna' in court circles) whose unfaithful husband—"fonder of girls than of gardens"—figures prominently in connection with so many pavilions. She amused herself with fishing and a telescope. "Depuis longtemps elle se conduit d'une manière édifiante." She went into exile in 1789 and the next owner was guillotined. In 1802 his widow (adopted daughter of Chalut) sold it to Napoleon's secretary, Bourrienne, who had it till 1816. From 1840–1895 it belonged to the Béarn family and now to the Noailles; (the Vicomte de Noailles is also the owner of Madame de Pompadour's house at Fontainebleau). The setting is perfect for a moonlight party, with the fountain playing in the 'bassin' and a ghostly ballet in the hornbeam trellis, a scenario of a Cocteau film too perfect, perhaps, to be worth doing.

70

71

The Château de Suisnes

The Château de Suisnes, in the Brie, near Grisy and Route No. 19 to Melun, is not the large building which existed till 1899 but a simple pavilion or 'vide-bouteilles' built in the middle of the seventeenth century for Nicolas Sainctot, maître d'hôtel du roi (Louis XIII) to which Mlle. de Vins des Oeillet, a tragic actress, retired during the reign of Louis XIV. In 1800 the Comte de Bougainville, intrepid admiral and explorer, settled down there and added three new pavilions, one with a four-columned garden façade back to back with the original. The architect was Bélanger, and his section includes a circular boudoir and a very grand columned dining room. The house is all on one floor. The little cour d'honneur is curved instead of rectilinear and contains statues in terra-cotta, the painted room is by Prince Henry XXIII of Reuss, a former husband of the last owner who was an American, the Countess Kotzebue. The interior has been charmingly reconstituted since the German occupation, and includes some boiserie in the salon from the Paar Palace in Vienna where Marie Antoinette was officially betrothed. More of this paneling is in the little salon of the Hôtel de Chanaleilles (q.v.). Besides giving his name to Bougainvillea, the Admiral introduced rose cultivation to the neighborhood. He lived there till his second son was drowned bathing in the Yerre which runs at the foot of the park. He died in 1811. In the eighties the Baron de Noirmont acquired the splendid park of Vernelle which adjoined the estate. Bougainville and Bélanger had already of course added grottoes and rocks to the old one and their 'salon de verdure' now contains a swimming pool. The park has many rare trees.

74

75

The Château de Jossigny

The Château de Jossigny, also in Brie, lies a few kilometers south of Lagny, thirty-four kilometers from Paris. Its entrance is on the village street. Neither too large nor too small, it is a dream house, occupied for centuries until quite recently by one family and almost unique in retaining its Louis XV décor quite untouched. If the Désert de Retz is Hafod (Wales), Jossigny is Up Park (Sussex). It is a provincial décor of the time, not grand luxe, and this is what has saved it. There may not have been fortunes to be made in parting with its furniture and paneling but nevertheless a strong temptation has been nobly resisted. The scarcity of Louis XV interiors is not entirely due to time and revolution—too often the rich were the slaves of fashion and redecorated in Louis XVI or even Empire styles of their own accord. The retort of Ledoux to the argumentative Elector of Hesse-Cassel— I see you are not rich enough to employ me—probably saved a great deal of lovely rococo in many a German principality.

At Jossigny the clock stopped about 1800; not an inch of wiring has entered. From 1574 the château-farm belonged to a legal family, the Bragelonnes. In 1743 their descendant, Claude le Comte, Seigneur des Graviers, constructed the present château (architect unknown). In 1940 his descendant's husband, the last owner, Baron Guy de Roig bequeathed it with its contents to the Beaux Arts together with the land to keep it up, and it is now open to the public from Saturday through Monday. The owner continues to live in the side buildings. The village postman (retired) shows you round. The family were great hunting experts, and the eldest son followed his master the Prince de Conti into exile at the Revolution, since when nothing seems to have been touched.

The wrought-iron gates are of the period; on one side is the chapel, on the other kitchens and orangerie. There is a Louis XIII bedroom, a Louis XV grand salon (illustrated), card room, music room, dining room (illustrated) with statues of Bacchus and Louis XIV cane chairs and a Louis XVI room completely furnished. The kitchen contains a ninety-piece 'batterie de cuisine' given by the Prince de Conti. There is also a 'salle de chasse.'

The gardens date from the earlier château and contain statues, a lime avenue, open-air theater and pleached hornbeam alleys.

The Maison Colin

The Maison Colin at the corner of the Rue Saint Louis and the Rue Royale, Versailles, was built for the Intendant of Madame de Pompadour, the central pavilion in 1746, the side ones six years later (1752). Colin inherited an earlier house there from his aunt and became the steward of Madame de Pompadour in 1748, when he was forty. He had already worked for her parents M. and Mme. Poisson, and was well liked and well thought of in Paris, where he gave up his position as procureur du Châtelet for the chancy but profitable post of assistant to the Favorite. At her death in 1764 he sold the house and returned to Paris. Meanwhile he had done it up with excellent taste and some of these decorations remain exactly as they were when Madame de Pompadour used to visit her private secretary. The high salon whose windows overlook both garden and forecourt contains boiseries of exceptional beauty. A lower room adjoining is adorned with chinoiseries in blue on a yellow background by Pillement, the chief introducer of the genre, whose work can be seen as far afield as Chatsworth and Beckford's villa of Ramalhao near Cintra. One of the panels is dated 1746. The garden is much smaller than it was originally when it vied with other 'jardins à la française,' that of Porchon in the Rue Notre Dame, and that of his employer the Duc d'Angiviller.

The Pavillon Colombe

The Pavillon Colombe in Sainte Brice near the Forest of Montmorency seems almost the ideal creation of Bélanger (yet it is not certainly his). Serene Gabriel, lofty and difficult Ledoux, delightful Bélanger—the friend of actresses, the husband of one, Mlle. Dervieux, and lover of another, Sophie Arnould. ("Mon bel ange," she always wrote to him)—his hand is in more gardens and pavilions than any other architect's, perhaps because he coincided with the wild outburst of building under Louis XVI, and with the craze for "romantic" gardens.

The Mlles. Colombe were three sisters of Venetian descent. Thérèse Théodore, the beauty, had a brilliant career in the Italian comedy, protected by the Duc de Richelieu, Adeline played soubrette parts and Mary Catherine abandoned the theater for galanterie. At one time she was arrested and found herself in the same prison as her original seducer, Lord Massereene. On her release she was anxious to settle down and went to live with Vassal, who had had the Pavillon Colombe built in 1769. The decorations went from gray to lilac and included charming allusions to her Italian origin—doves everywhere, Venetian mirrors and her initials, M.C. A place was kept for her portrait by Fragonard. When Vassal married he allowed her to retain the house during his lifetime.

She became the mistress of the Prince de Guéméné also and gave him back her jewels when he was ruined. Bélanger built a house for them on the slopes of Montmartre. She lived to be eighty.

The restoration of the pavilion began with Edith Wharton, the benevolent despot who bought it after the 1914 war (see Introduction) and who filled the little rooms she made with beautiful things. "The books seemed to snap back into their shelves on an invisible elastic," a friend told me. "No one fully knows our Edith," said Henry James, "who hasn't seen her creating a habitation for herself." She also laid the parterre, made the rose garden and the orchard of Reinette apples and luscious double cherries, all of which survive. She died here in 1937. Madame Saint-Rêné Taillandier raises a most interesting point in her comments on the Pavillon Colombe, which applies to other perfectionist proprietors (translation by Percy Lubbock). "Shall I make a confession? The perfection of her taste, extending to everything, even to the smallest details of her establishment, the arrangement of the flower-beds, the symmetry of the hedges, the neat ranks of the trees in the orchard—sometimes I was too conscious of it all, it chilled me. I have often noticed among Americans attracted by our civilisation and our traditions, something for which we ourselves are scarcely prepared, something that exceeds our measure. In nearly every French interior you will notice a clock that betrays the bad taste of the mother-in-law, or a wool-work chair-cover; touching relic of 'bonne maman.' With Mrs. Wharton I was intimidated by the aesthetic perfection of everything about her. . . . The society that surrounded her seemed to be composed of artists, writers, travellers, diplomats, people of culture—French, English and American—always a few at a time, without the added weight, never to be evaded by us in our homes, of family ties." *

I come down on the side of Mrs. Wharton after long reflection. If Mme. Saint-

* Percy Lubbock, *Portrait of Edith Wharton.* Constable and Co., Ltd., London; Appleton-Century-Crofts, Inc., New York. Copyright 1947 by D. Appleton-Century Co., Inc. Reprinted by permission of the publishers.

Rêné Taillandier feels intimidated, that's her lookout. Perfect taste always implies an insolent dismissal of other people's. It was to get away from her family and its nineteenth century belongings that Mrs. Wharton had settled in France in the first place. It was her misfortune to lack spontaneous gaiety and to be socially alarming and emotionally restless, qualities unfavorable to pavilion-haunting. Otherwise one would expect to see her ghost "with her broad-leafed hat and her basket on her arm, calling and waving to the window with her pair of toy-dogs scuttering and scuffling at her heels." "It was the time—wrote her friend—for the cutting of the roses of yesterday whose hour was over. Make room for today, for the red-streaked buds all ready for the sun—clip clip! The faded blossoms bent their neck to the scissors of fate and dropped into the basket." (Madame Taillandier)

The present owners, the Duke and Duchess de Talleyrand, have remodeled the interior closer to the original. In 1938 work was undertaken by the official government architect, J. C. Moreux. Mrs. Wharton was a perfectionist in living and the present owners are collectors, but also have children. There is a subtle swing over to Madame Taillandier's ideal and the house, while crowded with beautiful things, now breathes the "douceur de vivre" as befits the bearers of the name of the princely statesman who coined that famous but unverifiable expression. The salon is decorated with 'panniers de toile peinte à décor baroque,' the dining room holds part of the famous collection of Meissen birds and has twisted Venetian baroque pillars with vine motives. There are lovely Guardis and Tiepolos. On one side of the pavilion is a delightful orangerie, for the Duchess, an American, is as keen a gardener as Mrs. Wharton and is continually adding to it. "Pères de famille," wrote the Prince de Ligne, "inspirez la jardinomanie à vos enfants, ils en deviendront meilleurs."

The Pavillon de Musique de Madame

The Pavillon de Musique de Madame, Avenue de Paris, on the outskirts of Versailles, was long part of a larger estate, Le Grand et Petit Montreuil. The property was divided up and only the little pavilion survives. Marie-Josephine-Louise de Savoie, the wife of the Comte de Provence, brother of Louis XVI and afterward king as Louis XVIII was too quiet, even austere by nature to enjoy the frivolities of the Court. The château was rebuilt for her in 1780 with a 'hameau' copied from the hamlet of Marie Antoinette, an English garden with a lake and a river with islands joined by rustic bridges plus a temple and a ruin or two. The Pavillon de Musique was designed by Chalgrin and is a gem of Louis XVI architecture which we can still enjoy although the surroundings have been desecrated. The front is a low building of two small wings with a central pedimented hall projecting, approached by seven shallow marble steps. The *M* of Madame forms the chief decoration of the pediment. There are statues of Ceres and Pomona in the vestibule leading to the circular domed music room which is ornamented with Ionic columns and a fresco in trompe l'oeil whose fountains and arbors must once have existed in the park outside. A boudoir and a delicious octagonal salon with laurel wreaths in relief and Madame's monograms in Wedgwood medallions and a painted ceiling, complete the original ensemble with its many-mirrored doors and windows; the library and billiard rooms have been transformed. In 1789 the Comte and Comtesse remained in Paris and thence fled to England in June, 1791, the same night as his unfortunate brother set off for Montmédy. The Comtesse died at Gosfield in 1814. Montreuil was parceled up in 1793 and quietly stripped of its artificial simplicities. M. Chauchard acquired it some hundred years later as a retreat for old employees of the Magasins du Louvre, of which he had been one of the founders, and his frock-coated statue (1829–1907) then sat in front of the portico. Surrounding lotissements have now crept closer to these exquisite circular rooms. Chalgrin's original building of 1781 comprised only the central portion and very abbreviated wings. These wings were lengthened to include four more large rooms in 1825 and in no way detract from the harmony of the building. It was bought from the Magasins du Louvre in 1921 by M. Saintin and is now a sleeping beauty awaiting its prince.

The Pavillon de La Lanterne

The Pavillon de La Lanterne at Versailles, on the Route de Saint Cyr was once part of the Ménagerie (1662 onward) of Louis XIV. 'Lanterne' means a building one can see through. It is a two-storied building, designed by Le Vau, architect of Versailles and the Louvre, and reveals his great abilities. "Sobriété mais grande noblesse des lignes, avec les 'entrées' toujours traitées avec un soin particulier" (de Ganay). The two stags (much restored) on either side of the entrance are remains of the exquisite decorative sculpture which survives from the old Ménagerie for which Mansart built two pavillons in 1697. They have a faintly sinister surrealist quality emphasized by the zeal with which the casual observer is hurried about his business, for this most elegant pavilion is now government property. It was formerly in the possession of the American Ambassador, Mr. David Bruce, and is now a weekend residence of the French prime minister.

102

104

The Celle Saint Cloud

La Celle Saint Cloud, acquired by Madame de Pompadour in 1748 and sold in 1750 to the Fermier Général Roussel, was but a stage on her way to Bellevue, which the King inaugurated in 1750. The château, another 'lanterne' or transparent alignment of court and garden entrance, was begun in the seventeenth century by Joachim Sandrat, finished by the Prince de Marcillac and on June 19, 1659, Louis XIV and the whole court were received there. In 1718 the King's valet, Bachelier, acquired it. Madame de Pompadour enlarged it and Charles Colle composed his comedy *Henri IV's Hunting Party* there (1779). After the Fermier Général it became the property of Morel de Vinde. The Vicomte Morel de Vinde (1759–1842) (not to be confused with the famous theorist on gardens and enemy of the Anglo-Chinese fabriques [1728–1810]) was an agronomist and man of letters. Parliamentary councillor at the age of nineteen, he resigned when the King (Louis XVI) was arrested at Varennes, retired to La Celle Saint Cloud, and gave himself up to charity, literature and agriculture. Specimen titles—essays on the Morale d'Enfance, Le Morcellement de la Propriété, Les Constructions Rurales. He left behind happy memories of his profitable farming methods. Unlike most of these suburban domains, the château has retained its park.

La Maison des Musiciens

Originally the Pavillon Lemonnier, La Maison des Musiciens was built in 1755 for the Countess de Marsan, governess of the royal children. Louis Guillaume Lemonnier was the doctor to the King and a famous botanist and first formed, with his pupil Richard, the garden of Trianon. He became owner on the death of the Countess and lived on till his death in 1799. His widow kept up the grounds with their exotic trees, during her lifetime. Some of the first introductions from North America were made here. A few still remain. Here lived the Comtesse Guidoboni-Visconti (Frances Sarah Lovell) with whom Balzac fell in love at the height of his fame, in 1839. She was a cousin of the Queen of Beauty (with Madame Recamier and Madame Tallien) the Princess Belgiojoso. A Swedenborgian, Sarah Visconti may have inspired Balzac's *Séraphita*. She also sat for Madame de Mortsauf and Lady Dudley, and Balzac dedicated *Le Lys dans la Vallée* to her and also *Béatrix* before he was finally taken charge of by Madame Hanska. He is supposed to be the father of her son who died young. It is almost impossible to gain admittance.

The Pavillon du Butard

The Pavillon du Butard, a marvelous little building of tawny limestone, is one of the first of Gabriel's pavilions; it was built in 1750 as a royal hunting lodge in the Bois des Hubies, near the road from Vaucresson to Rocquencourt and was formerly beside a lake. The proportions are harmonious, the design extremely simple, relieved only by a pediment enclosing a wild boar being pulled down by hounds. The chief room is a circular salon two stories in height. There was also a 'cabinet de la chaise' and a 'rechauffoir' now used as a dining room, and a charming small staircase which leads to two bedrooms and an attic. In the basement a heavy arched pillar supports the salon above. The vestibule has a black-and-white marble floor. The oval salon has contemporary boiseries in two shades of gray with a frieze of cherubs and a blue ceiling. The garden side, which formerly overlooked the lake, includes the graceful five-sided curves of the octagonal salon. At one side of the approach are two buildings which it is interesting to compare, for these two staff cottages (shown here) date respectively from the eighteenth century and 1812 and their minor differences are revealing. After belonging to the Crown and the Empress Josephine the pavilion was let out during the nineteenth century and then became the headquarters of the Société des Vieux-Marly. In 1924 the Comte de Fels complained bitterly of the state of disrepair into which it had fallen. Later it was occupied by Georgette Leblanc, the friend of Maeterlinck. In 1960 it became the official residence of M. le Trocquer as President of the National Assembly and was the scene of the scandal of the 'Ballets Roses' when underage girls took part in strip-tease parties before the seventy-five-year-old statesman and his friends. An appropriate fate for the wanton King's pavilion—from the 'douceur de vivre' to the 'dolce vita.' Lost in woods, locked and guarded, it now seems to brood over its disgrace.

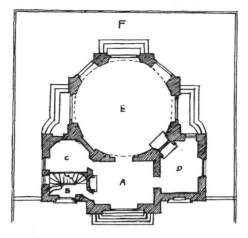

LE BUTARD

A VESTIBULE   D DINING ROOM
B STAIRWAY   E SALON
C CABINET DE CHAISE   F TERRACE

The Pavillon de la Muette

The Pavillon de la Muette gives a more genuine impression of being a hunting lodge and not a maison de rendez-vous, perhaps because it is bigger. (Muette means Meute, the Meet—which was held here at the double crossroads.) François I had built a hunting box here which Louis XIV demolished in 1665. Louis XV ordered its reconstruction in 1764 and the pavilion was used by him in 1768. He came and inspected everything on January 16th and on January 21st spent four hours in it since he could not hunt because the ground was frozen. In 1774 Gabriel was still working on it and in 1775 the paintings and mirrors in the salon were finished for Louis XVI. It was orginally planned to have a dome, a big square salon with octagonal rooms communicating. François I's cellars remain but it will be seen that the interior has nothing but its proportions of which to boast. The pavilion was reproduced in the French section of the international hunting exhibition at Vienna and is now an office and school for television operators.

"We arrived at about half-past one, or a little before, at La Muette, a small *rendezvous de chasse* with a few rooms in it, which were again all ready and prepared for us. . . . The dogs with the huntsmen were then brought up, and they played a fanfare on horns. Some *jeunes filles*, dressed all in white with green wreaths, then asked permission to present us with a nosegay and some fruit and they came accompanied by the curé. After this we took luncheon. The band of the *Gardes* played on the terrace in front of the house, and the huntsmen played fanfares. They are also dressed in dark green and gold, with red waist-coats and white gaiters. The Emperor gave us some excellent German beer." Queen Victoria's Journal, August 25, 1855.

118

The Hermitage of Madame de Pompadour

The Hermitage of Madame de Pompadour at Fontainebleau dates, like the octagonal Pavillon Français at Trianon, from 1748–1749. The Hermitage is near the park of the château from which it is separated by the Boulevard Magenta and can truly claim to be the first French neo-classical building, a foretaste of Trianon. The original plan shows a small central two-storied building with three high rectangular windows on the ground floor, square ones above, and a flat colonnaded roof enclosing an elliptical pediment (not triangular) with Madame de Pompadour's arms. On either side is a low one-storied pavilion with two rectangular windows below semicircular frames. All is immensely simple. Wings on each side were added at right angles along the forecourt and these now include a great many useful bedrooms and domestic quarters. Verberckt was in charge of the decoration. The whole was completed in eight months. At Madame de Pompadour's death it was repurchased by the King who gave it to the Marquis de Montmorin as a home for the Governor of the Château de Fontainebleau. During the revolution it fell into disrepair and was restored by Maréchal Bertier, Prince de Wagram. In 1921 it was bought by the Princesse de Poix, mother of the Vicomte de Noailles, the present owner.

The Hermitage is perhaps the most sympathetic of the pavilions in this book because it is not too close to Paris, has a large garden giving all-round protection, and is extremely well furnished with a charming feeling of an English country house, passages with shelves full of children's books or detective novels, bathrooms with mahogany baths and swan-necked taps, sitting rooms that are formal yet lived in. Everything suggests the somewhat Edwardian aura of the Princesse de Poix and the fastidious charm of its present owner who is president of the Société des Amateurs des Jardins. The gardens, besides some magnificent plane trees, include walled gardens with magnolias, camellias, albizzias and other tender plants, shrubberies, formal gardens with box and yew hedges, a well stocked 'potager' and an arboretum. It is the kind of garden where one is always stooping to read a label. Although not at all large and quite flat and bounded on one side by an important road junction, the division by hornbeam alleys into little sections—reminiscent of Hidcote—makes it seem bigger, and the view of the low wings of the house is always charming. Set well back from the road and approached by a fine gateway, it still does not prepare one for the riches within—the high library, the remains of Mme. de Pompadour's decorations on the landing upstairs, the salons and the many little bedrooms. There are some very fine screens, one in the smoking room in green-and-white chinoiserie, and the cornices and overdoors of the salon have retained their carving. One of the bedrooms has a superb parquet floor. Salon, smoking room, library and dining room have each their original atmosphere. Visiting it, one cannot fail to like Madame de Pompadour more and more or to envy the King slipping away from the hunt here to perform prodigies on his Sèvres chafing dish.

Gabriel also put up a little pavilion for Madame Du Barry in the Château of Fontainebleau which, on the accession of Louis XVI, was taken down with all its boiseries and the stones numbered. The Comte de Fels believed that this masterpiece might still be awaiting discovery in some local warehouse.

GAZON
dont la Totalité
jusqu'à la forest
est en petit en △

Voliere

Voliere

PAVILLON
de
M⁹ la Marquise
DE POMPADOUR
a
Fontainebleau

Basse cour

Ramuror

Chemin de Nemours et de Moret à Fontainebleau

Ecuries

PARC
du Chateau
de Fontainebleau

124

A Paris Sez le Rouge

du dessein de M. Lassurance Archi du Roi.

PLAN DE L'HÔTEL DE POMPADOUR, A FONTAINEBLEAU, D'APRÈS LE ROUGE

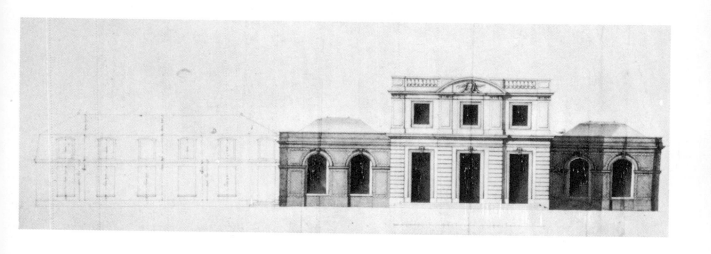

126

127

Pavillon Francais, Versailles

The Pavillon Français, whose picture in color is on our jacket, is in the center of the formal French garden, facing the Petit Trianon. A pure design of Gabriel it was built in 1750 for Louis XV and Madame de Pompadour, and was then called the "salon de compagnie et de jeu." It originally looked towards the greenhouses which were the King's great interest, but the view of these was blotted out in 1770 by the Petit Trianon itself.

132

The Petit Trianon

The Petit Trianon has already been partly described in the Introduction. It represents the true taste of Louis XV, who put in hours of consultation with Gabriel about it. Madame de Pompadour died in April, 1764, and did not live to see it completed. The building was begun in 1763, and was still unfinished in 1764. By September 10th the King was ordering the accessories. It was roofed by November and Guilbert had newly finished the stone-carving. The boiseries and indoor carving took from 1765–1768. It was not finished till 1769 and the King slept there on September 9th 1770.

The richest façades were designed to be seen by the King walking in the gardens. That on the side of the western formal garden has four Corinthian columns and a majestic double flight of steps; the northern, on the old botanical garden, has pilasters. The eastern, on Marie Antoinette's English garden, is plain, while that on the courtyard has pilasters again. Thus the most important façade is the left, at right angles to the entrance. Gabriel's eastern façade was not intended to face a 'jardin anglo-chinois,' but an inconspicuous area of the old botanical gardens. The beautiful proportions of the main floors and basement on the courtyard side are especially noticeable. The main staircase goes only to the first floor. The rich ironwork was added by Marie Antoinette, the lanterne by Lafont (1811), the antechamber looking on the courtyard and formal garden, was called the Salle des Poèles. The stoves (often masterpieces of rococo faïence) have disappeared. The main rooms are two dining rooms and the salon (originally a soft green) on the Jardin Botanique which are ornamented by garlands of flowers and pyramids of fruit. "C'est là, certainement, que l'art décoratif du XVIII siècle a crée son chef-d'oeuvre le plus parfait." (Comte de Fels) They form the joint product of Guilbert and Gabriel. Marie Antoinette's boudoir dates from 1787, a "décadence de goût" according to de Fels. The Pompeian documentation, he feels, has been insufficiently absorbed, and Mique here exhibits the sterility of the copyist. The Cabinet du Roi became Marie Antoinette's bedroom. There is some confusion about the location of his library and the "Pièce où est le caffé du Roi." The chapel, by Gabriel, dates from 1773 and was much damaged by damp. There are some remains of decoration in the attics, which once housed the Queen's visitors.

Marie Antoinette was just nineteen when Louis XVI gave her Trianon. "Vous aimez les fleurs, j'ai un bouquet à vous offrir." Mariolaters have described every nuance, every object in her occupation of Trianon. Her ghost has been seen in the park and there is a whole literature on the subject. In her dining room is a painting of her as a child dancing a ballet with her brothers, for it was thus she learned in Vienna her marvelous walk and deportment. "Vera incessu patuit dea." (Horace Walpole) Etiquette was relaxed at Trianon—the men went on with billiards or backgammon, the women with the piano or their embroidery when she entered. The delicate 'Pompeian' boiseries in the Queen's boudoir are by the younger Rousseau. The Queen's apartments overlooked the Jardin Anglais, a 'romantic' garden designed by the Comte de Caraman, her architect Mique and the royal gardeners Richard, father and son. They worked from 1774–1776. "Le beau rêve en effet," wrote the Goncourts, "ce palais et ce jardin enchantés où elle peut enfin ôter sa couronne, se reposer de la réprésentation, reprendre sa volonté et son caprice, échapper à la surveillance, à la fatigue, au supplice solennel et à la discipline invariable de sa vie royale, avoir la solitude et avoir l'amitié, s'epancher, se livrer, s'abandonner, vivre."

134

There were said to be eight hundred kinds of tree in her park including such rarities as the swamp cypress, the rose acacia, the Virginia live oak, and the sophora from China. It contains two remarkable little buildings by Mique, the Temple de l'Amour, like all 'temples d'amour' a copy of the temple of the Sibyl at Tivoli, open and circular, and the ravishing Belvedere. The god of love was a copy of Bouchardon's (now in the Louvre) and in the fêtes the temple was brilliantly illuminated across the water. Richard planted weeping willows beside it. The Belvedere was finished in 1781, an octagonal room guarded by six sphinxes. Lagrenée painted the ceiling and Leriche the walls in a style reminiscent of the Queen's boudoir—musical instruments, Pompeian arabesques, gardening tools, fishing apparatus, flowers, urns and emblems of love are painted on stucco and take us back to Nero's golden palace.

The theatre was built on the site of the old orangery in 1780 and has been restored to its original colours under a Rockefeller donation. It is richly decorated and some of the scenery of the plays in which the Queen acted (she played Rosina in the *Barber of Seville* by Pasiello) remain. In summer orange trees in tubs were put out round the Pavillon Français of Gabriel which had become the "salon de jeux et de conversation." The Hameau was the work of Mique and Hubert Robert whose great saying (he was imprisoned in the Terror) is not inappropriate. "Happy the man who can live philosophically in the memory of what he has been."

Napoleon gave Trianon to his sister, Pauline Borghese, while keeping Bagatelle for himself. In 1867 the Empress Eugénie began the collections of royal furniture and souvenirs of the unlucky Queen.

138

139

Bagatelle (Bois de Boulogne)

Bagatelle (Bois de Boulogne) was designed by Bélanger for the Comte d'Artois, then aged seventeen who had bet his new sister-in-law, Marie Antoinette, whom he wanted to impress, that he would have the place built and ready to receive her in the period between the Court's visit to Fontainebleau and its return to Versailles (sixty-four days). Or was the bet, perhaps, a trap to raise the money for the Folly? The first two days of September were enough to get the project started. Nine hundred workmen began on Sept. 23, 1777, and finished by November 25th at a cost of three millions, toward which the Count was helped by his wife. The 'casin,' as the Comte d'Artois called it, consisted of two vestibules, a circular salon between a boudoir and a bathroom, a billiard room and a dining room, and two small bedrooms, closets and so forth upstairs. The decoration was sumptuous—sculptures and decorations by Lhuillier, Pompeian arabesques by Dussault, and bronzework by Gouthière, whose chimney pieces still exist. It marks the next fashion to the Pavillon de Luciennes; the chiseled doorknobs with the monograms of Marie Antoinette are still in place and the panels in the little salon, by Hubert Robert with a profile of Louis XVI in the rocks of a grotto. The Count's bedroom was in the form of a rich military tent, its walls and ceiling draped in pale blue and white striped material edged with gold, the whole designed by Bélanger even to the clock. "La chambre à coucher du prince était à elle seule tout un poème." (Gailly de Taurines.)

After Lord Hertford bought Bagatelle in 1835 the rooms housed many of the treasures of his collection. Gainsborough's "Perdita" hung on one side of the magnificent four-poster with a melting Greuze on the other. The classical nudities were relieved of the whitewash which had covered nymph and naiad since the royal 'Retour d'Emigration' and there were gouaches of the original Bagatelle by Moreau le jeune.

After the death of the Marquis in 1870 his natural son, Sir Richard Wallace, inherited Bagatelle and marred the graceful proportions by raising the roof, but he did not spend nearly so much time there, though he too came back to die. His wife left it to his secretary Sir John Murray Scott, to whom she was devoted, who sold it to the City of Paris in 1904. It was fortified as a blockhouse in the Franco-Prussian War. The extraordinary claustrophobic atmosphere dear to the Marquis was perpetuated at Bagatelle by Sir Richard Wallace, although he was himself the most generous of men and one-time lover of Baudelaire's Madame Sabatier, la Présidente, whom he saved from want. Here is a description of one of his rare entertainments.

"My husband [Lord Warwick] was visiting Paris, and thought that he would like to see his old friend, so he wrote to his secretary, asking if an appointment could be made. In reply he received a letter saying that Sir Richard would be delighted if my husband would lunch with him on a date which he named, and still more pleased if he would bring with him Mlles. X and Y who, at the time, were the stars in the Paris theatres. My husband knew the ladies, so he passed on the invitation which was accepted eagerly.

"On the day of the luncheon, my husband and the two ladies drove to Bagatelle where they were received by the butler, who expressed Sir Richard's regrets that he was unable to welcome them personally, as his health was giving him great trouble. He added, however, that Sir Richard begged that they would do him the honour of enjoying the lunch that had been specially prepared for them.

"During the meal which was served in a small room like a study, something drew my husband's attention to a panel in the wall. As he was looking at it, the panel was slightly drawn back, and to his astonishment he saw Sir Richard's face appear! Sir Richard caught my husband's eyes but gave no sign of recognition. Instead he continued to stare fixedly at his guests. A few moments later the panel was closed as silently as it had opened. After lunch my husband and his guests left Bagatelle without having exchanged a word with their host. Lord Warwick never saw him again."

The gardens of Bagatelle designed by Bélanger were laid out (1778–1780) by the Scotch gardener Blaikie in the picturesque English style, with extraordinary 'fabriques,' a Pharaoh's Tomb, a Paladin's Tower and a Philosopher's Grotto, now disappeared. It was the most celebrated 'jardin anglais' of the time with a small formal garden in the very front of the pavilion. The entry was a Swiss chalet; the Philosopher's Grotto was Gothic with windows of different colored glass, to represent the passions. There were Palladian, Chinese and other bridges over the windings of the artificial river which became a lake with an island with the 'Tombeau du Roi de Coeur.' There were statues and vases, though not so fine as they would be in Lord Hertford's day. "C'est un désordre qui resemble à celui d'une coquette en négligé." The English garden, but with mid-Victorian arrangements, remains to this day with the famous rose garden of the City of Paris added. Before the last war a memorable exhibition of the rose in books and paintings (Redouté, Fantin-Latour, Ronsard, etc.) was held in the pavilion but now access is not so easy and its future is not determined.

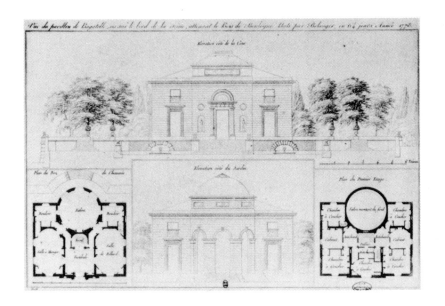

Le Comte d'Artois (Courtesy Musée d'Amiens)

144

147

Chambre à coucher de Monsigneur Comte d'Artois à Bagatelle Côté de la Croisée.

Chambre à coucher de Monsigneur Comte d'Artois à Bagatelle Côté de l'Alcove.

149

Cassan

The park of Cassan, near L'Isle Adam, was nearly wiped out in an air raid in 1945 but the pavilion, a reproduction of a Chinese building which was until recently used as a bathhouse, still exists. The original owner, Pierre Jacques Bergeret, had made a long journey in Italy in 1773 with Fragonard. Toward the end of the 1770's, he employed Morel, the author of the important *Théorie des Jardins*, an admirer of Walpole and Chambers, who gave free rein to his Anglophile ideas in the park of Ermenonville.

The building consists of a stout substructure of limestone and a superimposed, largely open, Chinese pavilion of wood, both with an octagonal ground plan. The inner room is circular, 2.5 meters in diameter, 3.65 meters high. It is surrounded by eight stone pillars with niches in the walls between. In the middle of the floor is a round basin somewhat below the level of the lake while a ring of Tuscan columns supports the low vault over the basin. All this is carefully executed in sandstone. On it rises the red and yellow painted pavilion, an octagonal room surrounded by an eight-pillared colonnade. Wooden bells were once hung from the projecting corners of the roof. The roof and its ornamental spire continue the pagoda effect. Of special beauty is the combination of Chinese motifs with a very close association between building and water reminiscent of the Nympheum of Chatou or the grottoes at Stourhead.

The Pavillon
Marigny Louveciennes

The Château de Louveciennes shown here for its 'Pavillon de Marigny' was bought in 1761 for his wife Catherine Ségent by the Comte de la Morière. Their daughter sold it to the Comte de Puy—the Comte d'Angles, Baronne de Montfauçon, Maréchal Magnan and Lemercier de Neuville take us down to 1893 when M. Emile Baillière bought it.

153

Chateau Du Barry

The Château Du Barry with another fifty acres of ground is now a separate domicile and belongs to Madame Papagos. It was originally built in 1700 to lodge the controller of the Machine de Marly (which pumped water up from the Seine). Later Louis XIV gave it to Madame de Toulouse; empty again in 1769, Louis XV offered it to the Comtesse Du Barry for her lifetime. She soon began to move all her treasures, especially her French eighteenth century paintings from her home in the Avenue de Versailles, and Gabriel drew up plans for enlarging the rooms. The salon and dining room received magnificent boiseries which still survive. It was here the jewel robbery took place in 1791. Subsequent owners included Spanish grandees, Salomon Goldschmidt and the Vicomte de Sartiges. There was also a 'Temple d'Amour' in the park and the existing ice-house in the Ledoux manner is interesting. Some of her jewels are supposed to be buried beneath a pyramid in the grounds.

155

156

158

Pavillon Du Barry Louveciennes

Since Eaubonne (see page 15), Ledoux had entered Court circles, perhaps through the family of the Duc d'Uzès or Thelusson, but he was in no way a rival to Gabriel of whose Place de la Concorde he wrote "c'est là, c'est dans ce fastueux édifice que brille le sentiment inépuisable de l'Architecture Française." He was, however, destined to become the architect in fashion until his arrogance and lofty imagination set him too far above the gay young Anglo-maniacs like Bélanger. But that day lies ahead. "En regardant le plan de ce pavillon," writes J. C. Moreux of Louveciennes, "les yeux aussi bien que l'esprit éprouvent un plaisir profond, une véritable délectation." It indeed is frozen music, and there is a design of Ledoux's for the façade suggesting that he used the methods of composition by geometry and number dear to Vitruvius and Palladio. A drawing in the Albertina shows us its original appearance (before an extra floor was added), but with the Seine flowing past its door! "The Lodge" (according to Pidansat de Mairobert) "is square-shaped with five windows on every side. It is situated on a considerable eminence, whence is enjoyed one of the most gorgeous and extensive views possible. The river, winding about the foot of the hill in the form of a horseshoe, contributes not a little to adorn this scene. In front of the house is a courtyard, perhaps too vast for the building, the entrance to which is supported by four plain columns in antique taste; the entrance is ornamented with a bas-relief by the Sieur le Comte, representing young bacchanals. The interior consists of a hall for dining, with a service room on the left, and a cloak-room on the right, and a parlour with two drawing-rooms on either side. There are no bedrooms. In the hall are four small boxes for the musicians belonging to the Countess, as she has had for some time her own band. There is an inconvenient sameness in the distribution of the whole that does no honour to the invention and taste of the Sieur le Doux. The most celebrated artists have endeavoured to enrich this delightful residence with their labours. The ceiling of one of the side-rooms was executed by Bisard. Its motto is *Ruris Amor*. It depicts pleasures of the country. On the other side is painted a hazy sun and four large pictures by Fragonard, which describe the amours of shepherds and seem to be an allegory of the adventures of the mistress of the house. They are not yet finished. There are some fine pieces of sculpture; they are as yet but models, and are to be executed in marble. Art, however, appears to have less exerted itself here in grand masterpieces than in miniature ornaments, such as chimney-pieces, fireplaces, sconces, girandoles, chandeliers, cornices, gilding and goldsmith's works, locks, bolts etc., every part of which is so exquisitely finished that they might all be exhibited as models of perfect workmanship. . . . The general impression produced by the view of such a contrast is that we are in the house of a kept woman, every part of which betrays the owner" (English translation, 1777).

The author was evidently ignorant of the Bibliothèque Infernale, the exquisitely bound collection of erotica which is almost Madame Du Barry's only masterpiece not to have ended up in the Louvre. The decoration was above all the triumph of Gouthière. The dining room was in gray marble with gold Corinthian capitals on the pilasters, and the chairs were by Cagny with tapestry seats by Tripperet. The 'Ruris Amor' salon was paneled in mirrors.

Madame Du Barry took her coffee there when she returned to the Château Du Barry under Louis XVI. She was arrested in 1793 and the pavilion set off on the inevitable downward course until the banker Laffitte acquired it in 1818. Through the nineteenth century it had many owners. Most of the original decoration disappeared. M. Alfonse de Rothschild bought the Gouthière pilasters from the salon with their female figures. In 1929 M. Coty the then owner began excavations underneath to install a kitchen, fur-storage rooms, servants' rooms and a swimming pool. The whole building began to fall in. At a cost of nearly a million dollars he had it rebuilt according to Ledoux's plan and all the fixtures copied, but the architect, Mr. Charles Mewes, had to choose between making the rooms smaller to allow modern heating and wiring or enlarging the building while keeping Ledoux's relative proportions. He chose the latter and the building as we see it is really a reconstruction, and the inside a replica with all the original decoration copied except in the entrance and dining-room. It is no longer classified as a historical monument by the Beaux Arts. "It has no value at all," said an official, "like your Williamsburg." During the war German officers lived there and the concierge, Madame Petit, saved what she could. It was recently sold with ten acres and now belongs to the American School in Paris. The salon is a cafeteria full of coat-racks and formica tables. A fragmentated statue of the Du Barry survives in the garden.

162

Elevation du Côté de l'Entrée.

Elevation du Côté de la Rivierre.

1 2 3 4 5 6 7 8 9 10 Toises

Coupe sur la ligne A. B.

Plan des Souterrains.

Office de Travaille

Office

Cuisine

Office

Dégagement

Dég.t

Lavoir

Bucher

1 2 3 4 5   10 Toises

Plan du Rez-de-Chaussée.

Jardin.

Boudoire

Salon

Salle de Jeu

Jardin.

Antichambre

Salle à Manger

Dég.t

Cabinet

Portique

Grande Cour.

Dessiné par Krafft

Boudron et Boulay Sculp.

163

164

The Pavillon Du Barry

The stables and house of Madame Du Barry in Versailles (3 bis Avenue de Paris) are now the Chamber of Commerce. In 1751 Binet, premier valet de chambre of the Dauphin built a 'pavillon bâti à la romaine' here which Madame Du Barry acquired in 1772. She asked Ledoux to add stables and offices along the Rue de Montbauvon and a gateway on the Avenue de Paris where her arms were sculpted by Lecomte between figures of Flora and Minerva, Flora being supposed to represent Madame Du Barry. The gate remains but the arms are changed. It recalls Ledoux's porch for the Hôtel de Hallwyl in Paris. His original plans for the stables (1773) were worthy of Pegasus or of the Condés at Chantilly but they were simplified and watered down and have gradually disappeared like most of his work, the larger part of which in any case never left the drawing board like "Le généreux projet de ta vaste cité."

> Là serait le bonheur; là, de la race humaine
> Le monde eût admiré le plus beau phénomène. . . .

But enough of conditionals: Madame Du Barry entertained lavishly in the Pavillon Binet but after her disgrace in 1775 it became the property of the Comte de Provence (Louis XVIII) and her possessions were removed to Luciennes. More stables were built which were used for cavalry and the name was changed to that of his first écuyer, the Marquis de Montesquiou. Its subsequent occupants were the military until 1899 and it was reconverted into a private house by M. and Mme. Huard in 1923 until the illustrator of Balzac sold it to the Chamber of Commerce in 1937. It is partly furnished with objects of the period and the garden façade and staircase retain their old charm.

168

169

170

The Château de la Chesnaie

The Château de la Chesnaie at Eaubonne near Montmorency is one of a group of buildings attributed to Ledoux who designed some houses there for a rich family of Fermiers Généraux, the Lenormands de Mézières (1767). There were also some twenty lesser houses forming the street which ran as far as two small pavilions, entrances to another mansion, now demolished. The houses are not as interesting as Ledoux's later work and take a good deal of sorting out, for in 1776 he returned to Eaubonne and built (again for M. Lenormand) the Petit Château, a beautiful little cubic Palladian building quite emancipated from the Boffrand influence in his houses of ten years earlier. Eaubonne had a romantic past, for Madame d'Houdetot had a house there while her husband and lover were both away in the army in Germany (1757) and Rousseau wooed (and won) her from his hermitage at Montmorency under the celebrated acacia tree. Her accepted lover, Saint Lambert, the cold and unlikable philosopher lady-killer who had caused the death of Voltaire's Madame Du Châtelet by making her pregnant, also had a house there on his return. (We meet these members of the Montmorency set in the scene at La Chevrette described by Diderot in the Introduction.) M. Vacquer in his splendid *Anciens Châteaux de France* gives Saint Lambert one of the Ledoux châteaux, the Propriété Dumont, now destroyed. He traces the 'Petit Château' of 1776 through General Comte Merlin, the Comtesse d'Haubersart, the Tarbé des Sablons, the Langlois families and finally M. and Mme. de Chabert in 1911. The main façade maintains its antique grandeur. The less attractive 'grand château' is now the Mairie and already spoiled.

The château de la Chesnaie belonged to M. Goupy who died in 1793. It is now the property of M. Jacques Dupont and was restored in 1941 by the official architect, M. J. C. Moreux, specialist in Ledoux and author of the commentary in the fascinating book on Ledoux published by the Arts et Métiers Graphiques in 1945. The château is two-storied and nine-windowed according to the regular formula, with a pediment in the middle, and a terrace on the garden side. M. Moreux removed some Second Empire verandas and interior coatings of chocolate varnish. The seven-windowed salon although of 1767 is in pure Louis XVI. The Aubusson carpet is late eighteenth century. Another Aubusson covers the tile pattern of the dining room with its original marble pilasters, its chairs by Jacob and candelabra by Gouthière. There is a beautiful staircase, a small paneled dining room and a columned hall.

173

174

The Désert de Retz

The Désert de Retz (six kilometers from St. Germain at Chambourcy) has been called the most interesting building of the eighteenth century (Comte de Ganay) and was also one of the most admired at the time. The little park and everything in it are a splendid hymn to ruin, an elegy on dead fashion, the main building is one of the most beautiful and original designs for living one could imagine, a perfect merger of classical with romantic. It consists of a truncated fluted column the top of which was once slanting and irregular and which has since been flattened down, though still on a slant, with three floors inside and four rooms on each, grouped round a shallow spiral staircase. The windows within the fluting of the columns are rectangular on the ground floor, square on the first and oval on the second. The top floor was without windows and was lighted from the roof but at a later date some windows were added. The diameter was about fifty feet, the column about eighty feet high. According to the Prince de Ligne it resembled a "fragment from some colossal building which like the Tower of Babel had provoked the wrath of God," and indeed it is a little reminiscent of the painting by Altdorfer. The name comes from the old French word 'essarter,' to cut wood, and 'res,' the local word for king, the land being part of the forest of Marly which was then a royal domain.

The proprietor and architect and designer of the Désert de Retz was a rich dilettante, 'huissier de la chambre du roi,' the Chevalier François Racine de Monville, who built it in 1771. He was clearly an Anglomane and a person of considerable talents and exquisite taste for he had to solve difficult problems of design in his oval and circular rooms, and in the placing of cupboards and passages. The house was so well furnished that the State confiscated most of his best pieces after the Revolution which he, although a close friend of Philippe-Egalité, adroitly survived. * He was known to be a harpist, a sportsman, a botanist, scientist, and most proficient archer, "the best archer in France, perhaps in Europe," who could bring down a partridge with his bow and arrow. In fact, with his republican leanings, and wide knowledge he seems a typical English dilettante of the late eighteenth century, a beckfordising Walpole worthy, with a touch of romantic paganism, like Richard Payne Knight. Did he visit England? And was his taste for ruins philosophical like Diderot's or purely aesthetic—or as Miss Rose Macaulay hazards—a symptom of sexual frustration? He was undoubtedly helped in the layout of park and 'fabriques' by Hubert Robert, painter and 'dessinateur des jardins du Roi' (his best known gardens were Méréville and Rambouillet). The grounds were sloping and ir-regular, enclosed by a wall (some of which remains), and were entered by a frowning Mycenaean portal in a rock. Le Rouge, in his *Jardins Anglo-Chinois*, shows an engraving of this 'natural' entrance with two statues of fauns (or servants disguised as fauns) brandishing a torch in each hand and lighting the way to some sinister nocturnal fête. The

* "The news of the manifesto of which he was the object reached home when he was at dinner, tête à tête with Monville, a man of wit and pleasure. 'It is appalling, Monseigneur,' replied Monville without disturbing himself as he finished squeezing the juice of a lemon over a sole, 'But what do you expect? They have got all they could out of Your Highness, and they treat you as I treat this lemon.' And Monville burnt the peel in the fireplace, adding that soles should always be served piping hot."—*Memoirs of Lauzun*

Monville-Robert out-buildings of this Parisian Hafod include (or included) a pyramidal ice-house like a tomb from the Appian Way, a ruined Gothic chapel, a tomb, a hermitage —one of these is a 'petit autel ruiné' and a Temple of Pan (still fairly intact) in the north-west corner. The only building not designed as a ruin but completely decorated and furnished was the five-room 'Maison Chinoise,' now, largely because of the American G.I.'s quartered there in the last war, in a state of irremediable disrepair. Its chinoiserie was copied from ornamental drawings rather than from buildings, "un modèle en recherches" according to the Prince de Ligne. By 1808 the whole place was out of favor and the Comte de La Borde dismissed it as an example "du mauvais goût qui régnait à cette epoque." The Chinese pavilion is later than that of Chambers at Kew and is like those painted on chinoiserie coffee pots and tea caddies of the late seventeen-sixties. In the tower, in summer, exotic house plants filled all the niches on the spiral staircase. Two hundred more flowerpots were hung round the outside of the column. The unusual trees planted by M. de Monville, "bon dessinateur, bon architecte, bon jardinier, bon botaniste" (J. C. Moreux) now run riot over the tangled wilderness. * Its decay is due to a succession of Philistine owners who included an Englishman, Disney Ffytche or Ffytche Disney (1792–1827), under whom it was badly kept up, and from 1856 the Passy family. Though classified by the Beaux Arts in 1939 it is in a terrible state today and from the rooms scrawled with graffiti chimney pieces have a way of disappearing. It is a tragedy that no one has ever come forward with the means and taste to restore it. I visited it with the late Christian Bérard one afternoon in 1945 and fell hopelessly in love with it. Mr. Zerbe remembers it in 1949 with goats clattering up the beautifully modulated spiral staircase. The new owners who may yet halt the demolition are M. and Mme. Courtois.

In nearby Chambourcy is the tomb of Lady Blessington and the Regency Dandy Count d'Orsay who rest in that same equivocal proximity which they maintained during their lifetime.

* The Scotch gardener Blaikie takes a less charitable view—perhaps he was envious. "The Duke (of Orléans) had many of these pretended connoisseurs about him. . . . M. de Monville was frequently of his party and a Pretended Connoisseur in everything; he had formed a garden and Path according to his own designs adjacent to the Forest of Marly where he had made his Château in form of an old round tower with a Staire in the Middle surrounded with flower-pots which made a tolerable agreeable effect; the Appartment was small all around the tower from the staircase; the top of the Tower seemed to have been ruined—I cannot think but he meant to emulate the Tower of Babel. He had some good Hothouses and by them he had a little Chinese pavilion where he generally lodged."

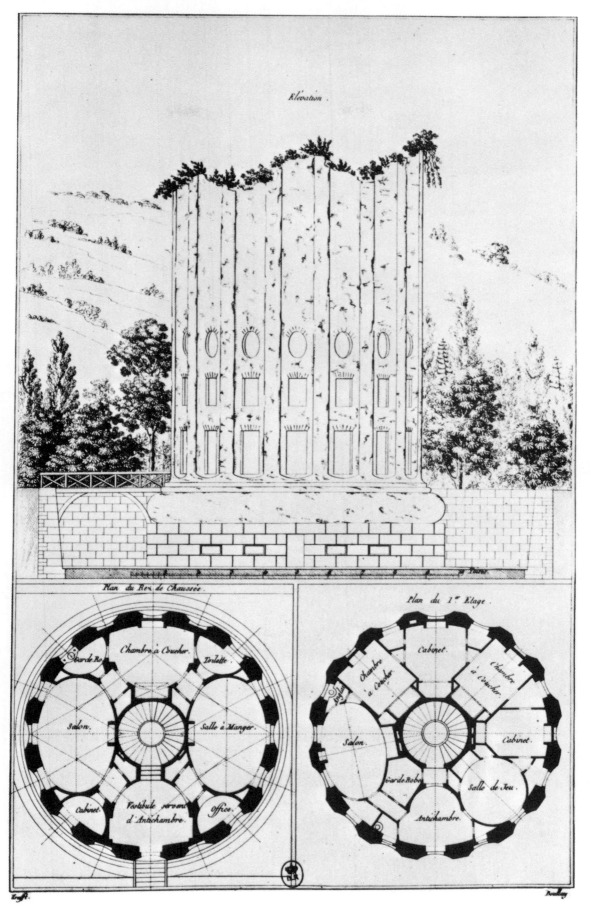

Elevation.

Plan du Rez de Chaussée.

Garde Ro.

Chambre à Coucher.

Toilette.

Salon.

Salle à Manger.

Cabinet.

Vestibule servant d'Antichambre.

Office.

Plan du 1.er Etage.

Cabinet.

Chambre à Coucher.

Chambre à Coucher.

Anglais.

Salon.

Cabinet.

Garde Robe.

Salle de Jeu.

Antichambre.

179

183

Coupe de la Maison Chinoise sur la Largeur en Face du Jardin.

La Maison Chinoise vûe du côté du Couchant.

184

The Folie Saint James

The Folie Saint James (Neuilly), 16 Avenue de Madrid, as we now see it "assez maltraitée à la Libération par les Américains et laissée à l'abandon par son propriétaire," according to Pillement, and practically inaccessible as well requires a certain effort of the imagination. It is easy to glimpse its harmonious façade across the courtyard and we can spy a small circular temple in the garden which is surrounded by apartment houses. The garden front has a three-arched central veranda and a double flight of steps. Yet it once deserved eighteen plates in Krafft and its garden was famous. The house was built in 1774 by Bélanger for Claude Baudard, Baron de Saint James, Trésorier de la Marine. After his bankruptcy in 1787 it was inhabited by Wellington, Chateaubriand and Thiers among others. The park once extended to the Seine and contained famous statues by Lemoyne and Pajou. The interior retains some pleasing decoration, but like the Pavillon de Musique de Madame at Versailles, the site has been terribly overbuilt. Here Bélanger designed for Boudard de Vaudésir, Baron de Saint-Gemmes (anglicized to Saint James) in 1784 the last of the "Anglo-Chinese" gardens (the Chinese Pavilion was destroyed by a shell in 1870). They were not unlike the gardens at Monceau which Bélanger had laid out for the Duc de Chartres (the Folie de Chartres [destroyed] as opposed to Bagatelle, la Folie d'Artois). On a cart dragged by forty horses an enormous rock was brought from the Forest of Fontaine-bleau, out of which a river was made to flow from a Doric façade in the rock, reminiscent of Stourhead. The rock was a mass of grottoes and exterior paths and contained a sumptuous bathroom (total cost 600,000 francs). The serpentine meanderings of the river were crossed by a variety of bridges. There was a 'Pont d'Amour' leading to an 'Ile de Magnolias' and a 'Pont Sphinx.' Under the lake an underground maze was laid out with a small Gothic dairy. A glass temple held a 'collection of minerals, rare birds and crustaceans' and was converted into a chapel. It survives, like the great rock and its temple and one of the beautiful stone bridges.

It is worth pursuing the Baron de Saint James, "The Man with the Rock" as the King nicknamed him, a little further. He has an engaging, if slightly weak face. In 1772 he bought the property for 400,000 livres and asked Bélanger to put up anything he liked "pourvu que ce fut cher." (How different from Ledoux's niggardly patrons.) Saint James was "stout and fat, of medium size, very red in the face with that freshness of complexion one can still have at fifty if happy and in good health." After sixteen years of enchantment in his Eden the unfortunate Saint James lost a million in speculation and was unwittingly involved financially in the scandal of the Queen's necklace. The Comte d'Artois regarded this rival in extravagance with no friendly eye and urged Bélanger to ruin him, while making disparaging remarks about the sources of his revenue to the King, his brother. Saint James retired, at his own request, to the Bastille where he died in 1788, still bankrupt because he was owed a large sum by the Government and the 'folie' went to the Duc de Praslin. The Duchesse d'Abrantes (1808) owned it and described it as 'cette ravissante maison—un très beau salon et une grande salle à manger avec un premier salon servant de salon de musique.' Madame Recamier lived there, aged sixty-five, in 1842. The photos of the interior taken for Vacquier's book in 1913 reveal the most delicious Louis Seize plaster-work in the salons, a fine staircase and a columned hall with huge vases and life-size statues painted in trompe l'oeil; the interior of the 'chapel' is also decorated. The 'folie' is now a school.

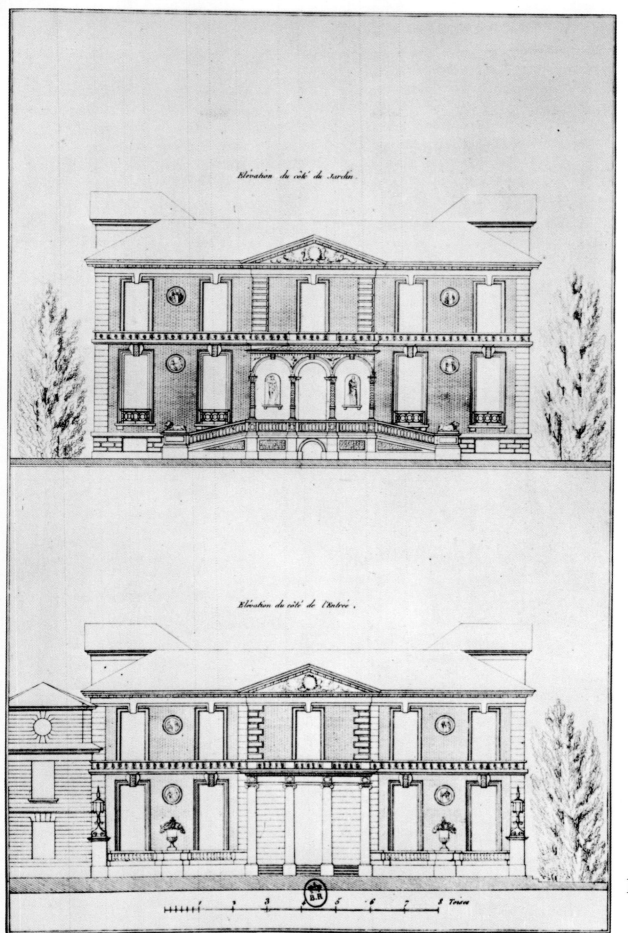

Elévation du côté du Jardin.

Elévation du côté de l'Entrée.

1   2   3   B.R   5   6   7   8 Toises

189

The Hôtel de Jarnac

The Hôtel de Jarnac, 8 Rue Monsieur, was built for Leonard Chapelle in 1783 to the plans of Le Grand and then rented to the Comte de Jarnac from whom it took its name. It is a typical town house with courtyard and garden, ground floor, first floor, and attics, with circular buildings on each side of the main block, and a particularly impressive gateway. Both the fine façade on the street and the humbler one on the garden were much admired, the latter especially from the courtyard of 39 Boulevard des Invalides. There were decorations in the style of Clodion and a figure of Fortune in a square panel in the dining room. The Grand Salon, with its reliefs, was particularly magnificent, with the Elements in the "Dessus de Portes." Today the house belongs to Madame Meunier of the chocolate family, who also owns Chenonceaux.

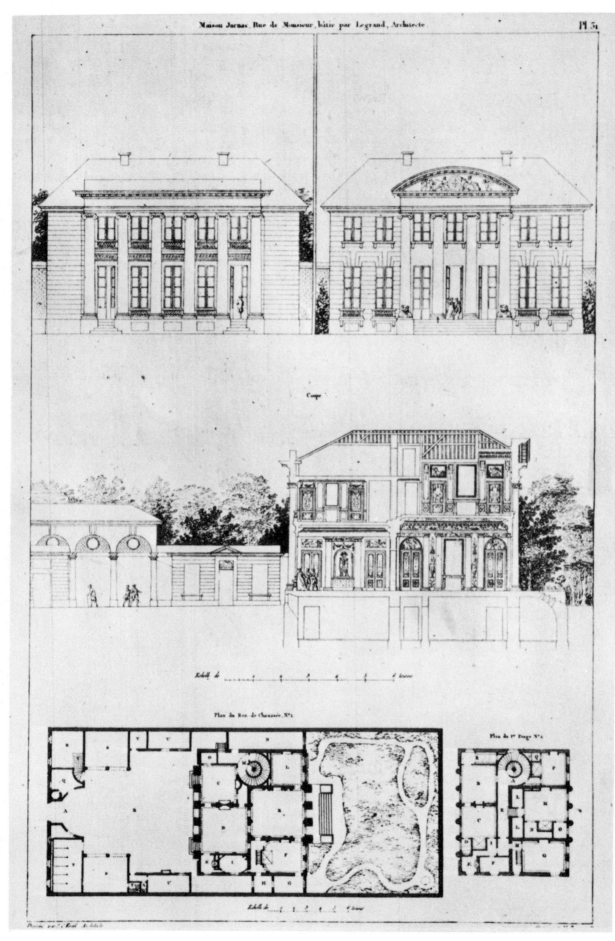

Coupe

Echelle de

Plan du Rez de Chaussée. N°1

Plan du 1er Etage N°2

Echelle de

195

The Hôtel Turgot

The Hôtel Turgot is almost surrounded by a modern apartment house in the Boulevard Saint Germain. The garden façade, which is well above street level, still exists (the garden overlooks the Rue de l'Université). On the street is an inscription that here in 1781 died (of gout, aged fifty-four) the Baron Turgot, the brilliant minister of finance of Louis XVI, who tried to save the finances of the tottering kingdom. The house belonged to an American, Mr. William Gower, when these photographs were taken.

198

The Hôtel Gouthière

The Hôtel Gouthière, 6 Rue Pierre-Bullet, was built from 1772–1780 for the bronze-worker Gouthière who had to sell it because of his debts in 1787. It is one of the most charming Louis XVI exteriors we possess and reminds us of several that have vanished. The sphinxes by the steps, the doorway arch where two seated genii crown a divinity and the bacchic procession of children in the bas-relief after Clodion above the door make us feel as if we are entering a Roman temple. The back is more conventional and disappointing but the interior has retained some of its decoration. There is a salon with Pompeian arabesques entirely covering the walls in high rectangular settings. Two more downstairs rooms are in the Empire style and there is another Louis Seize room on the first floor decorated with pastoral scenes in medallions. Surrounded by warehouses, with a fire station at one side, the pavilion is not easy of access. Its fate was perhaps decided by the inability of the Court to pay its craftsmen so that outstanding excellence, from the Boulle family onwards was sentenced to bankruptcy.

Pierre Gouthière (1732–1813) was the son of a saddle maker. By 1758 he was working in Paris and married the widow of his master, François Ceriset, master gilder. The marriage brought him Ceriset's shop, La Boucle d'Or, on the Quai Pelletier. In 1764 he was among the creditors of the great silversmith F. T. Germain whose bankruptcy should have been a warning. Put not your trust in princes! By 1769 he was collaborating with Bélanger and others in the famous jewel cabinet for Marie Antoinette. He worked for the Royal Palace till 1777, especially for the Duc d'Aumont, the Comte d'Artois and for Madame Du Barry at the Pavillon de Luciennes. In 1788 he was declared bankrupt. The Revolution completed his ruin. After the Revolution he vainly sued the heirs of Madame Du Barry for 756,000 francs. Although he was the finest craftsman of his time, works authenticated by him are very rare. There is no proof that he ever combined with Riesener.

The hôtel is now a fringe maker's workshop.

La Petite Malmaison

The Empress Josephine received as many gifts from Napoleon as if she had been a Favorite. (The centerpiece of her silver-gilt dinner service, by Biennais, adorns the dining room of the Hôtel de Chanaleilles.) Like Madame de Pompadour, whose garden at her Hermitage in Versailles was so famous for its scents that it could be visited at night, she was greatly attached to exotic plants and built rows of enormous hothouses at Malmaison for the encouragement of new importations, roses above all, which from 1803 she employed Redouté to paint for her. Even as the Malmaison carnation was famous, so were the 'old-fashioned' roses, the Bourbons and Bengals that she cultivated. Near her hothouses she decided to build a 'folie' as somewhere to serve tea to her friends before they made the obligatory tour. The pavilion with its long white façade was designed by Berthault and survived the war of 1870, but the park was divided up in 1878. The present owner is M. Czarinski. The round entrance hall has a fine parquet floor with arabesques picked out in black, and leads onto a large and beautiful music room with white-and-gold furniture, rose-patterned Aubussons, and mahogany torchères, a study in gray-and-white trompe l'oeil on a green ground, a small salon with delicious Empire ornamentation, blue silk walls and gilt laurel wreaths. Behind the clock, reflected in an 'enfilade' of mirrors, can be seen the photographer with his faithful Rolleiflex.

The Empress acquired Malmaison in 1798 from M. Le Coulteux de Molay, himself a gardener. Berthault laid out the enlarged gardens, Lenoir designed some 'fabriques' and obtained the statues including a colossal Neptune by Puget. Besides two hundred and fifty kinds of roses, she acclimatized hortensias, hibiscus, dahlias, camellias, catalpas, mimosas and rhododendrons. The large planthouse rivaled Kew and Schoenbrünn. In 1800 a cedar was planted near the château to celebrate the victory of Marengo. Isabey, the 'Hubert Robert of the period,' also advised. Many garden experts were consulted who contradicted each other. The Empress would not permit a single straight line.

The Villa Trianon

The Villa Trianon at Versailles (Boulevard Saint Antoine) was the home of an American lady who unlike Edith Wharton can never be reproached with too glacial a quality of heart or head, the celebrated interior decorator and hostess, Elsie de Wolfe (Lady Mendl). Its story is best told in her own words.

"Whilst we were living in the little house we used to walk along the Boulevard de Saint-Antoine, pausing to peer through the iron grill of an old deserted villa which stood so lonely at the corner . . . the more Elizabeth [Marbury] and I though about the old house the more excited we grew about it. Scarcely a day passed that we did not dream of possessing it. At last we prevailed upon the house agent to let us have the key. We were entranced by it. The house, unlived in as it had been for decades, spoke to us with regret and resignation of the passing of an old grandeur. For it had belonged to the Duc de Nemours, the son of Louis Philippe. And the outbuildings had been part of the *hameau* of Marie Antoinette." They bought it in 1906 for 16,000 dollars.

"A clause in the deed, dating back to 1750, reserved a right-of-way through our garden for all time to the King of France. Getting ready to restore the villa we consulted Monsieur de Nolhac, the conservator of the Château de Versailles. Monsieur Nolhac placed at our disposal the original plan of the house as it had been a century and a half before. Elizabeth put the repairs and their supervision entirely in my own hands. For twenty-seven years and more I have never stopped planning. Today I look upon it as an artist may look on the masterpiece to which he had devoted his best efforts. If I have done anything really fine it is the Villa Trianon."

There was only one bathroom in the sixteen-room villa. Miss de Wolfe and Miss Marbury put in six and bought from Lady Anglesea (an American) some blue-and-white boiseries for the two salons and the 'Mille Graces' curtains for the dining room. This lady (Minna King of Georgia) had bought for her villa (Madame de Pompadour's Hermitage) the Pavilion de la Rotonde from the Palais Royal, and the complete Art Nouveau room exhibited by the Bonne Marché Store in the Exhibition of 1900 which was installed in her Versailles salon. A terrace was built along the garden front; a statue by Clodion, a parterre, clipped yew pedestals followed and in 1909 came the Music Pavilion by M. Duchesne. It is octagonal and contains the parquet from an old château, beside it is the blue-tiled swimming pool. In 1909 a party arranged by Boni de Castellane was given for the crown prince of Greece, with a dinner for sixty on the 'tapis vert' and the 'cors de chasse' of Versailles making melancholy music. After the First World War the large terrace opening on to the gardens was glassed in. The vegetable garden became famous. With the death of Miss Elizabeth Marbury the villa became Lady Mendl's and she entertained here all through the thirties, giving a celebrated 'murder party' for Daisy Fellowes about which Henri Bordeaux wrote a novel. The villa now belongs to her neighbor, M. Paul Louis Weiller. I have quoted from her autobiography *After All*.* Her biography has subsequently been written by one of those who fell under her spell as an old lady, Mr. Ludwig Bemelmans. Mr. Zerbe's photographs were taken in her lifetime. The frescoes are by Drian. "You are not a modern woman," Monsieur de Nolhac often said to her. "You are a ghost who has come back to us from the Court of Louis XV." In her refusal to grow old and show worry or bad temper, that is what she was. She taught café society to stand on its head and to avoid soup. "I do not believe in building a meal upon a lake."

210

* Harper & Brothers, New York; William Heinemann Ltd., London.

214

Le Noviciat

Le Noviciat also belongs to M. Paul Louis Weiller, who built it in the twenties. It stands on the edge of the Park of Versailles, near the Villa Trianon. Its approach is slightly sinister for one passes along the ivy-clad walls and northern fir trees to face a hole in the wall of the porch through which the Germans covered every arrival with a machine gun. It was Goering's headquarters for a time during the war. At one side is a deep concrete shelter. The garden front is cool and stately, there is a rather large garden with fine hedges, lawns and statues abutting on the immense timber of the park. The opulent period interior is unemphatic but we can see the books placed sideways to show their armorials in the circular library, and in the salon is some of the actual parquet from Versailles once trod by so many tiptoeing feet and acquired for Le Noviciat when the floors of the palace were relaid.

Le Pavillon Lopez-Willshaw

Le Pavillon Lopez-Willshaw, 4 Rue de la Ferme, Neuilly, was orginally built in the early nineteen hundreds by M. Rodocanachi, from whom his friend M. Arturo Lopez-Willshaw acquired it and by whom it has been largely rebuilt about 1923. It is the most dazzling recreation of the age of Versailles that I know and some may prefer it to its rival the Hôtel de Chanaleilles because the pictures are contemporary with the furniture and because of Mr. Lopez's personal audacity of taste, a flair which suggests an uncanny confidence in his knowledge of the period. The house is full of 'serendipity' as Walpole called the gift of discovering unexpected associations. Returning after the war, M. Lopez acquired a perfect model of the wedding of Louis XV in colored 'verre de Nevers.' This magic congregation, the King and all his Court in church, is another of those extraordinary scenes which one can seem to penetrate; it is suitably enshrined and lighted. Madame de Pompadour's microscope is another haunting object. Authenticity reigns in everything, this is no decorator's pastiche.

In this small and inconspicuous pavilion, with a courtyard and a garden front overlooking a rectangular pool is housed a Louis XIV arrangement which must be unique outside a royal château. A balustrade shuts off a 'lit de parade' from the rest of the salon, with its magnificent savonnerie carpet. In one corner is a portrait of Madame de Montespan, a bust of Philip le Beau and a portrait of the Duchesse de Bourgogne. The models for the decoration of this room are from Le Brun and Le Vau. The Louis XIV bed is covered with Genoese velvet and a royal Gobelin of Louis XVI is hung behind it. The dining room contains some treasures of French silver-gilt which are to be found nowhere else, a surtout by the fabulous Meisonnier, vessels by François Thomas Germain, a hunting centerpiece of hounds and boars and cors de chasse by him and matching candlesticks representing shaggy forest trees. There is a very large silver-gilt service of Catherine the Great's. Some of this silver, including a rococo coffee pot for the King of Portugal (F. T. Germain, 1756), a covered dish and sugar sifter, Strasbourg, late seventeenth century, and two German candlesticks are illustrated in color in "French Art of the 18th Century" (*Connaissance des Arts*). The Germain hunting trophy (destined for the Louvre) was shown in the Munich rococo exhibition. A secret padded treasure chamber which is also a safe contains a collection of Renaissance jewelry and rock crystal. Upstairs a comfortable modern salon provides a living room and in the basement are ornamented shell-grotto rooms for large parties. There is an accent on Régence and the early rococo in this pavilion which makes a pleasing break with the Louis XVI prevailing in so many others. Note the beautiful porcelain stove.

It was a pleasure to watch Mr. Lopez setting off in his black red-lined cloak with his finely pommeled cane and an enormous diamond ring which belonged to Louis XIV, on his gloved hand. He reminded me both of Monsieur, Louis XIV's brother, and again of the Louis XV Comte de Breteuil, according to which reign he was reincarnating.* I am reminded of a letter from Walpole to Montagu written from Paris in 1767, a rallying cry for all pavilion lovers.

* A British ambassador described a visit to the newly opened rooms at Versailles with M. Lopez who insisted on being the last of the party to pass through every door. "C'est qu'ici je me sens un peu chez moi." A faithful copy of a Louis XIV suite of solid silver furniture and a grass garden theatre are among the latest additions.

"Visions, as you know, have always been my pastures; and so far from growing old enough to quarrel with their emptiness, I almost think there is no wisdom comparable to that of exchanging what is called the realities of life for dreams. One holds fast and sure to what is Past. The dead have exhausted their power of deceiving."

231

The Hôtel de Chanaleilles

When I first saw these words on a gatepost one summer evening in the thirties the house behind seemed to sum up the spell of the Faubourg Saint-Germain. "Sacred names, Rue de Chanaleilles. Summer night, limes in flower; old houses with large gardens enclosed by high walls, silent in the leafy heart of the faubourg. . . ." I wrote seven years later, "Sensation of what is lost"—and when I revisited Paris at the end of the war the house still stood shuttered and silent. Now it has become the most talked-of interior in Paris, the home of M. and Madame Niarchos and their dazzling collections, an example of that fantastic luxury within the reach of the twentieth century which, when combined with the collector's fever, creates an almost stifling richness of texture, a sensation of nervous excitement as if life must never for a moment fall below an impossible level in these surroundings where every picture, object or piece of furniture and even the cushions and curtains could be in a museum. Such interiors as the Hôtel de Chanaleilles or the Pavillon Lopez-Willshaw are by the addition of modern heating and lighting, superior in 'luxe, calme et volupté' to those of Madame de Pompadour, Mme. Du Barry or Bagatelle and they create a feeling of suspense; only a revolution, the deluge, or the head of the Duc de Brissac lobbed through the window—"de la chute des rois funeste avant-coureur"—is worthy of them; the rest is anticlimax; they are like the mirage of Valhalla burning at the close of Götterdämmerung. Yet that sensation, too, is part of the mirage for there is no reason why they should not outlast us all.

The hôtel, as we see it today was built about 1770, from a hunting pavilion of the previous century, a 'folie' of the Duc de Maine. At the time of the Revolution it was the home of the Marquis de Brabançon. Under the arrangement for the confiscation of émigrés' property it was won by a Madame Bonnat who sold it to Barras. The story goes that the financier Ouvrard went to see it with Madame Tallien one winter's day in 1799 who said, "It is lovely. Happiness must live here" and that the same day he sent round a small gold key in a bouquet of roses with a note "there is the key to your house." It was then called the 'petit palais de Babylone' and had a much larger garden, indeed a park, like its neighbors the hôtels de Biron, de Rohan, and de Matignon. Madame Tallien, daughter of the Spanish banker, Cabarrus, had been taken before the terrorist proconsul Tallien at Bordeaux after being captured trying to escape to Spain. He fell violently in love with her and she used her influence to save many of his victims, thus hastening his recall to Paris where before he could be punished, he was instrumental in overthrowing Robespierre, and so releasing her from prison. It was then they got married. After her divorce from Tallien she married the Comte de Caraman, afterward Prince de Chimay, and died at Menars in the château which had been the home of Madame de Pompadour's brother, the Marquis de Marigny. This beautiful and generous woman queened it for many years in Revolutionary Paris, although Napoleon would not receive her; she died in 1831. Barras was her old lover when he sold the pavilion to Ouvrard who was her new one. She had four children by him. She covered the colonnade from the street to make an extra room for parties and laid the marvelous floor which Napoleon coveted, and put in the bath which can still be seen. The Marquis de Chanaleilles bought it in 1840 and M. Niarchos in 1956. M. Emilio Terry was the architect employed in the final reconstruction, and he solved both the inevitable problem of pavilions—how to install some bedrooms—

and a special one—how to include some Régence panels in a room twenty centimeters too low for them—by rebuilding the whole wing. By excavating all the earth which had been deposited by the floods of 1907, the garden was lowered and the basement, hitherto practically walled up, was exposed, thus bringing to light Madame Tallien's delicious Pompeian bathroom with its sunken bath and frescoes.

The Hôtel de Chanaleilles is T-shaped, the crossbar being the covered-in colonnade now part of the new entrance. With its wonderful wooden mosaic in rare woods and the breath-taking, flame-yellow curtains and row of four crystal chandeliers, it is one of the most beautiful empty rooms (one daren't call it a passage) in the world. It leads to the red salon with Corinthian columns and gilt ceiling and red velvet walls where hang a Goya and a Seurat and the famous "Pietà" by El Greco. A Savonnerie with the royal arms, a gift of Louis XV for the King of Poland, covers the floor and the furniture includes an ebony writing desk with mounts by Gouthière. "I don't want my house to be a museum," explained M. Niarchos, "nous voulons une maison vivante." "J'aime les teints fraîches, vives, jeunes," added Madame Niarchos, who must have been echoing the wishes of Madame Tallien. In the newly reconstituted wing is a boudoir with exquisitely carved white and gold boiseries from the Paar palace in Vienna, where Marie Antoinette was betrothed, and its appropriate Renoir, and then the big salon with its gorgeous lacquers, the only room to preserve the character of the mid-eighteenth century with its swelling commodes and Louis Quinze chairs. On the other side of the T beyond the red salon, is a white salon, with a Gauguin, and the dining rooms (one for the children). The principal dining room has another wonderful parquet floor (Mme. Tallien's) and two Degas dancers on its original paneling and here is displayed some of the Puyforcat silver. (M. Niarchos bought the whole collection when it came up for auction and presented it to the Louvre, retaining only some Empire silver-gilt vessels for his temporary use.) There are at least six Renoirs as well as van Goghs and other Impressionists, some Rouaults, a blue Picasso, a Lautrec of Bruant, a Degas doll, a Corot portrait (above a cabinet by B.V.R.B.) —and also a quantity of fantastic china—Meissen, Sèvres, ormolu-mounted objects and Chelsea tureens. "The unity is in the quality." I am not myself altogether happy with the theory that eighteenth century décor and nineteenth and twentieth century painting go so well together. Most of the painters here represented would turn away in disgust from the lavish artificial frivolity of eighteenth century decoration. They were not like Henry James who "could stand a great deal of gilt" and they deserve to be worshiped, not merely admired. But they are perhaps happier here than with Mr. Edward G. Robinson, in Hollywood whence—en bloc—fifty of them came. The eighteenth century came to prefer wall decoration and boiseries to paintings, and tended to use painters more and more for small panels or dessus-de-portes. To hang such walls with Cézanne and van Gogh is to diminish their beauty and also to deny the revolutionary quality of the paintings, which were in the artists' opinion dynamite.